Praise for *Powered by Honda*

Powered by Honda is a must-read for all executives concerned with their firm's survival and success.

David N. Burt, Ph.D.
Professor, Supply Chain Managment, and
Director of the Strategic Supply Managment Forum
University of San Diego
Co-author, *The American Keiretsu*

Powered by Honda tells the story of what Honda does by the people who do it. You can hear the belief and commitment behind their actions. With this book you experience the power of a unifying vision, unswerving support, deep human understanding, and the guts it takes to implement effectively. I knew they were good—but now I know why.

Rick Dove
Chairman, Paradigm Shift International

The relentless challenge of continuous improvement is jolted forward from time to time by special contributions from outstanding leaders. David Nelson and the wonderful team he assembled at Honda of America have made such a contribution. *Powered by Honda* will impact gobal competitiveness far beyond the auto industry.

Mike Doyle
President, Doyle Consulting Group
Chairman & CEO of The National Initiative for Supply Chain Integration, Ltd. (NISCI)

Powered by Honda is the inside story of Honda's BP program for enterprise excellence and is the best program of its kind in the United States.

Robert W. Hall
Founder, Association for Manufacturing Excellence
Editor-in-Chief, *Target*

Powered by Honda is for every leader's desk. If managers apply what they read in this book, their organizations will be dynamically improved, and their customers, along with their associates, will be delighted.

Robert A. Kemp, Ph.D., C.P.M.
President, National Association of Purchasing Management
President, Kemp Enterprises
Professor Emeritus, Management, Drake University

Powered by Honda tells the compelling story of how to improve buyer/supplier relationships and mutually benefit from breakthroughs in supplier productivity. A must-read for executives and professionals in supply management.

Robert M. Monczka, Ph.D.
Director, Professor of Strategic Sourcing Management, and The National
Association of Purchasing Management Professor, Michigan State University

Powered by Honda is filled with valuable insights and uncommon sense. It is an excellent resource for managers who want to achieve world-class performance in their own organizations.

Richard J. Schonberger
Author of *Building a Chain of Customers*
and *World Class Manufacturing—The Next Decade*

Conventional widsom is to slash, bash, and wire together a chain of lowest bidders for improved results. Honda and Dave Nelson provide a model company and a roadmap for enlightened supplier–managment relationships. *Powered by Honda* proves that suppliers of choice willingly provide preferential support to a customer that earns trust, respect, and demonstrates flawless performance.

Ken Stork,
President, Ken Stork and Associates

For those who think of Toyota as the leader in lean thinking, here's a colorful explanation of how Honda's "racing spirit" is creating a truly lean enterprise in North America. Nelson, Mayo, and Moody provide a step-by-step plan for building a smoothly-flowing value stream from raw materials into the arms of the customer. Anyone who can't follow their simple instructions (and who doesn't get on the case immediately after putting this book down) has little chance of staying in the race.

James Womack
President, Lean Enterprise Institute
Co-author, *Lean Thinking* and *The Machine That Changed the World*

If you are in management, you must read this book. It reveals the inside details about BP, Honda's famous management technique that slays even impossible challenges and works lightning fast.

Willard Zangwill,
Professor, University of Chicago

POWERED
BY
HONDA

DEVELOPING EXCELLENCE
IN THE
GLOBAL ENTERPRISE

POWERED
BY
HONDA

DEVELOPING EXCELLENCE
IN THE
GLOBAL ENTERPRISE

DAVE NELSON
RICK MAYO
PATRICIA E. MOODY

JOHN WILEY & SONS, INC.
New York • Chichester • Weinheim • Brisbane • Singapore • Toronto

Published simultaneously in Canada.

This publication is designed to provide accurate and authoritative information in regard to
the subject matter covered. It is sold with the understanding that the publisher is not engaged
in rendering legal, accounting, or other professional services. If legal advice or other expert
assistance is required, the services of a competent professional person should be sought.

Library of Congress Cataloging-in-Publication Data:
Nelson, Dave, 1937-
    Powered by Honda : developing excellence in the global enterprise
/ Dave Nelson, Patricia E. Moody, Rick Mayo.
      p.   cm.
    Includes index.
    ISBN 0–471–18182-X (cloth : alk. paper)
    1. Honda Motor Company—Management. 2. Automobile industry
and trade—Production control—United States. I. Moody, Patrica E.
II. Mayo, Rick, 1957– III. Title.
HD9710.U54A636   1998
338.8'87292'0973—dc21   97-45106
                                                  CIP

Printed in the United States of America.

10 9 8 7 6 5 4 3 2 1

Contents

Dedication

Dave Nelson: To George A Harris, V.P. Materiel, TRW, Inc. (retired),
my mentor and my friend.

Rick Mayo: To my Dad for his wisdom, to my wife Rita
for her patience and support, and to my son Cody
who gave me the energy.

Patricia E. Moody: To Molly Sherden, who made it all come together.

Ackowledgments

"In a race it is the teamwork between the driver, the mechanics and the engineers that generally determines success or failure. If the mechanic fails to do his job, the driver has no chance. If the engineers fail to design the car properly, the mechanic has no chance. All are dependent on each other."

—Mr. Shoichiro Irimajiri, former president of Honda of America Manufacturing, in his speech to the Harvard Business School in 1989, "The Racing Spirit."

Our crew has many team members, and we thank them all for getting us to the track on time, prepared, and ready to seek the challenge:

Kimmie Ball, Leilani Benton, Doug Chamberlain, Dave Curry, Steve Francis, Mike Goddard, Richard Harrison, Larry Hopcraft, Bob Hust, Susan Insley, Barbara Kavanagh, Tom Kiely, Dave King, Roger Lambert, Mary from Batesville, Mississippi, David Schaefer, Peter G. Schmitz, Rick Schostek, Ruston Simon, Jon Stegner, Cheryl Stillings, John Wright.

Introduction

C an you imagine all of your suppliers, in every commodity, delivering each part on time, every time?

Or if you are the plant manager or the head of a small or medium-sized supplier to a big customer, would you like to have a proven way to raise your productivity, improve quality, and cut waste—all without paying big consulting fees? What about having a mechanism that brings out all of the power and expertise of the best experts in production—your employees—to achieve even higher quality and production performance?

Sounds aggressive? Sounds like massive culture change? Think again, because this simple, proven approach from Honda called *BP* (Best Position, Best Productivity, Best Product, Best Price, Best Partners) has for over twenty years revolutionized the way companies operate. Starting with critical suppliers in Japan and moving to North America, the United Kingdom, and Europe, Honda BP has moved from first- and second-tier suppliers into the third tier. Major producers, such as Parker Hannifin, Donnelly Corporation, and TRW, have made BP their own.

What does it take to seize the opportunity? Honda BP was developed by the great sensei Teruyuki Maruo, who taught the next generation of BP experts by taking them out to the shop floor, to the actual spot, to see the actual part, to evaluate the actual situation. No off-site million-dollar training programs, no outside million-dollar consultants running amok in your plant. BP just requires focus, commitment, and management support. Fewer than a dozen simple techniques will help your employees themselves learn how to see, hear, and gather data and solve the problems on the floor. All they need is the opportunity and some help from those who have already been there.

THE GAME OF CORPORATE CHICKEN

When David Halberstam predicted in his 1989 landmark book, *The Reckoning,* that the automotive world would experience tremendous upheaval in the 90s, he foresaw a dangerous supply/demand imbalance—five cars for every four buyers—a buyer's market. That imbalance is playing itself out in a game of corporate chicken in which none of the players wants to back down. The strategies for capturing finite demand include competitive pricing, product innovation, aggressive marketing, and the power of customer loyalty.

The first approach to capturing demand is competitive pricing, which is completely dependent on the automotive assemblers' command of over 5,000 components supplied by internal and external producers. At Honda, about 80 percent of the vehicle comes from Honda suppliers who hold the key to customer satisfaction. Further, big cost and quality opportunities lie with second-, third-, and fourth-tier suppliers.

Halberstam's demand/supply imbalance will continue to take its shakeout toll as various players struggle to keep up the pace or just stay in the race. GM and Volkswagen will attempt to leverage cost cuts on the backs of suppliers, Saturn will attempt to occupy a narrow niche, while Cadillac will sell pedigree. Toyota, with its deep pockets and continued dedication to lean manufacturing systems, will continue to be one of the strongest competitors.

THE BEST TEAM WINS

The winners will be those few automakers who design well and fast, giving maximum attention to customer fulfillment, who deliver lower sticker prices, whose quality maintains zero defects, and whose strategy is to design and produce where they sell. Clearly, the best customer/supplier teams, the best extended enterprise, will win.

In 17 years, Honda of America Manufacturing (HAM) has built an integrated supplier network—Honda's extended enterprise— that is positioned to take competitive advantage of excellent, committed suppliers, combined with superb logistics and innovative information systems. *Powered by Honda* takes a dynamic look at how Honda of America matured from a tightly controlled transplant dependent on Japan for components, design, and direction, fighting to gain a North American foothold, to an automotive giant noted for its aggressively creative growth strategy.

One of the auto industries' most demanding customers, Honda exports U.S.-built cars and parts to over 60 countries around the world, with new plants coming on-line in Canada, South America, and Europe. Total parts purchased in 1996 of $4.6 billion, from 353 suppliers, will exceed $5 billion. Now focused on introducing new product lines, including the first North American high-end luxury car, the Acura, designed and produced by Honda, the company's position has become one of an innovation leader whose strategy is to design, source, and produce where they sell.

CORPORATE STRATEGY LEVERAGES THE SUPPLY BASE

How has Honda built a supply base whose partners consistently deliver zero ppm defects, with to-the-minute on-time deliveries, at very competitive costs? Dave Nelson, senior vice president and a member of the HAM Board of Directors, points to the company's demonstrated execution of corporate strategy through a single driver—the purchasing function—grounded on the idea of developing, rather than leveraging, excellent suppliers.

"HAD ENOUGH OF PICOS?"

Other producers are taking a different road to excellence. GM has PICOS. Ford, Chrysler, Nissan, and Toyota all subscribe to their own supplier development systems. But suppliers, the experts who supply over 80 percent of components, prefer the Toyota and Honda systems. A philosophy-driven approach combining classic quality analysis and problem-solving techniques, superb communications and people skills enables repeated BP successes. Three simple diagnostic and problem-solving tenets guide day-to-day operations:

1. Go to the spot—one can only diagnose and fix a problem by "going to the spot" (the shop floor) to talk with the experts;
2. Build the foundation; and
3. Bet on the process.

YOUR GUIDE TO BP

Use this book to envision the possibilities. Imagine your people, empowered and energized, taking *your* company into the era of the lean enterprise. Think about the importance of management commitment to letting BP perform its magic. And remember, the magic is that there is no magic at all.

1

Rocio's Story

S he is working hard. This is a new job for her, and it pays well. She assembles and tests automotive component assemblies at a small plant in Reynosa, Mexico.

Rocio holds a master power window switch for a Honda Accord in her right hand. With her left hand, she orients a connector and plugs it into the bottom of the switch. Then she changes hands, and touching the assembly the way a driver would, she activates the four switches, one by one. She cycles the buttons with her thumb, while with her right hand she cycles the test board on and off. She watches the indicator lights, looking for good connections, or occasionally, intermittent flashes that would mean, to the customer, intermittent problems.

Perched on a stool at the end of the assembly line, Rocio, and thousands of workers just like her, performs these repetitive movements dozens of times per hour, hundreds of times per day, thousands of times each week. Sometimes her shoulders ache from bending over her test table. Sometimes her wrists hurt from manipulating hundreds of small components. Sometimes the part passed to her by her upstream neighbor doesn't work. But always, Rocio quietly keeps up the pace.

Is There a Better Way?

At this TRW plant, something new is going to change the way Rocio and thousands of associates just like her in other plants worldwide do their jobs. Two visitors from Ohio, Tom Kiely and Steve Francis, have arrived to introduce Honda's powerful supplier development program, BP, to this and hopefully other TRW plants. Their plan? To give the Reynosa workers, whom Honda calls associates, a way to take control of the production process with which they work, to raise their own quality and productivity levels, to make their jobs easier and physically less taxing, and to help them prepare for the incredible growth opportunities coming their way as a key Honda supplier.

The BP Program is a very simple 13-week, hands-on process that Honda has perfected and applied in over 120 successful projects to help achieve tremendous productivity improvements. Some of the 90 companies have, in turn, applied the BP process to their own suppliers. It's a many-tiered web of production success stories.

BP stands for Best Position, Best Productivity, Best Product, Best Price, and Best Partners. It is a very powerful continuous improvement process designed by Honda experts that can revolutionize the way companies raise their performance levels. BP builds stronger processes through eliminating waste and accessing the creativity and intelligence of associates. The BP process is based on the principle that the production experts, the associates who perform the work, are the greatest source of improvement ideas and creativity.

BP works with a range of industries—from plastics and stampings to electronic assembly and weldings—with all types of employees. The process unlocks productivity potential as it produces significant, permanent culture change through workforce training and development, and employees' invaluable participation in the process.

BP is not a consultant-driven process. Companies who volunteer to begin the program draw on expert help to learn and perfect the process and to select and launch projects. Honda BP team members help teach the process, but the hard work of change falls to supplier employees and managers themselves. Enthusiastic testimony from hundreds of energized employees reinforces the impressive BP results. BP is a transforming experience.

Like all Honda initiatives, BP is a philosophy-driven approach based on a few powerful but simple continuous improvement techniques, combined with energized employees and partners, that attack basic process issues. BP addresses a broad range of areas, from soft-side issues, such as housekeeping, ergonomics, work flow, and

Figure 1.1   BP, Honda's Powerful Supplier Productivity Development Program

Launch date:	1976 in Japan, 1990 in North America
	90 companies — 120+ projects
Supplier associates affected	120,000 in North America
Productivity gains overall	47%
(total pieces per man per hour before BP compared to pieces per man per hour after BP)	
Quality improvement overall	30%
Cost-down overall	7.25% overall

BP, as well as other Honda improvement techniques (such as Value Analysis and Value Engineering) helped reduce the actual cost of purchased parts for the 1998 Honda Accord by more than 20%. These savings were generated not from cost avoidance, but from actual savings in material and labor of purchased parts.

other noncapital equipment-driven improvements, to higher investments relating to tooling and major equipment changes. Phase 1 BP attacks housekeeping, ergonomics, work flow and other noncapital equipment-driven improvements; Phase 2 BP addresses bigger, more expensive equipment changes.

One other outstanding feature of Honda's approach to supplier improvement is that the suppliers *themselves* make the changes, with

Figure 1.2   What is the BP Project?

WHAT IS THE BP PROJECT?

WHO   One to three Purchasing Support and Development associates and two or more supplier associates

WHAT   BP is a voluntary project, using the focused team approach, to teach Honda's suppliers the continuous improvement philosophy.

WHERE   At the supplier's facility

WHEN   The project can be conducted over a 12-month period. The first 13 weeks are intensive with two to three days a week spent at the supplier; the last nine months are follow-up with once a month visits the norm.

WHY   Status quo and complacency will ensure that you are falling behind the competition.

HOW   Using simple BP techniques

help and guidance from Honda associates who pitch in; but when the 13 weeks are up, the suppliers are running the show. The program creates supplier self-reliance.

Steve Francis and Tom Kiely have been sent to Rocio's plant. They know that they are facing a tough challenge. Reynosa has been showing irregular delivery and quality performance as other TRW upstream plants miss their schedules; TRW and Honda execs are worried.

Kiely and Francis have asked for TRW high-level support and demonstrated commitment. They want engineers from other TRW

Figure 1.3 Why BP?

WHY BP?

- 80 percent of Honda of America Manufacturing parts are purchased from supplier base.

- Suppliers need to be healthy, strong, and competitive with their entire product line in order for Honda to remain competitive.

- Improve the working relationship.

- Improve quality to customers.

---

facilities to learn the process. Francis and Kiely are hoping to train the future trainers, but first, the performance problems must turn around. Their task is being monitored at the highest levels of Honda and TRW.

How It All Started—BP at TRW

In response to Honda's measured feedback on quality and delivery problems, TRW executives announce that they want to be the number-one supplier for their product line. Honda Purchasing's reply is, "If you want to be number one, we need to build our relationship and learn to work together to meet or exceed our expectations. We want you to consider a BP project."

Seven TRW sites had been considered. Honda Purchasing management evaluated each opportunity, trying to pick the ones that showed the most opportunity for improvement. BP gurus Steve Francis and Rick Mayo (*Powered by Honda* co-author) visited a half dozen TRW North American plants, and at each one they evaluated performance from a BP "opportunity" standpoint, using empirical data wherever possible, as well as visual observation of plant housekeeping and personnel, and a third factor—their "gut." They settled on Reynosa because it was the last stop on this product's assembly schedule, and people said it would be the most challenging. And more importantly, Honda needed the parts. Reworking parts and incurring further schedule slippage might have worked for some companies, but Honda felt that reworking parts to make today's shipments would not solve tomorrow's problems. Rework is not cheaper and does not train the workforce in permanent solutions. Honda manufacturing veterans knew that reworked parts could eventually shut down their lines. They wanted a permanent fix.

Taking any improvement program into a supplier plant is a challenge. Management may decree the change, but the employees must live with, execute, and deliver results. And the employees understand this. For the Reynosa project, Tom Kiely was chosen to work with Steve Francis who had been working in BP for three years and had completed 7 projects to Tom's 10. They had worked together on a tough stamping project and felt they knew the territory. However, neither of them spoke Spanish.

Francis and Kiely made weekly trips to Mexico, where they joined other BP team members, including three other TRW engineers—Betsy Granger, a line-production supervisor from the Auburn, New York, plant; Kim Ott, an industrial engineer from Marshall, Illinois; and Steve Murphy from the Farmington Hills, Michigan, office—along with two Reynosa associates—Francis Escamilla and Hector Rodriguez, the only bilingual team member. Quite a team! No shared experiences, no trust, and no common language!

At week 3 in their 13-week program, Francis and Kiely were still making trips to the plant. Travel costs were piling up—airfare, food, and lodging. Quality and delivery problems persisted. Line workers were paid, parts or no parts. Red ink on the production control white board fed frustrations as the tally of shortages and unbuildable assemblies mounted. Whenever BP team members approached the line, workers stopped talking and averted their eyes.

AND THEY KEPT ON SMILING

To these workers, Kiely and Francis were, as manufacturing supervisor Hector Rodriguez remembers, "just another parade of visitors, a charade."

"We used to joke about the 'parade,'" recalls Rodriguez, "the parade of improvement programs marched through our plant, and we even threatened 'no new ideas until we know that new visitors are coming!' because we knew that that was the only time that support management, like maintenance, or engineering, would help us out. We were jaded."

Francis and Kiely had introduced themselves and set up a suggestion box in the middle of the production line. Each morning Kiely "emptied" the box, pantomiming a weeping engineer as he turned the box upside down and shook it—no suggestions. They had feared that associates would not trust them, and they were right. Why should they? Rodriguez met Kiely's "Introduction to BP" speech with an experienced warning: "Nice try, guys, but this will fail too." But Kiely and Francis just smiled. Plant supervisors asked, "Why are you smiling? You are going to fail. You are in a different world here. Maybe this would work at Honda, but not here. I will see you, before three months are up, return to Honda, frustrated."

And they just smiled.

Just Give Us Six Weeks

Francis made a proposal. "Give us six weeks and you'll be convinced. We've heard this before, but in six weeks, you'll see results." Rodriguez raised his hand and volunteered six weeks, knowing "they wouldn't last six weeks here. They'd be gone the first month...."

You Could See the Gleam in Their Eyes

The Honda team decided to go one on one with line workers. Their first customer was Rocio. The workers were shy, and they knew that whenever they had a good idea, an engineer would steal it and pass it off as his. Kiely remembers, "They thought we were just there to give it to them in the ribs."

"We had ideas," says Francis, "but we wanted them to come from the associates. *We* knew how to speed and balance the line, but the improvement had to come from them." The team was looking for a quick hit, that day if possible.

Rocio seemed approachable. Francis and Kiely asked if she had any ideas that would make her job easier. She acted as if she didn't understand. The Honda people spoke only English, and she knew they would not be around long enough to learn Spanish.

But in a small whisper, Rocio told Hector, "I want the test fixture angled so I can see the lights better." This was their first suggestion! She left for lunch, and the team got to work.

In the back of many small plants, there is a scrap pile filled with corrugated cardboard, wood pallets, and scrap metal. Kiely and Francis paw through the junk, looking for a way to follow through on their first inroad. Kiely spots it first—a small chrome magazine rack, the wall-hanging type.

Thirty minutes later the new test fixture is in place, and Rocio returns from lunch. The team hides in the BP room, watching

Rocio's face through the window blinds. She starts to smile...."The Honda visitors had listened!" Rocio's expression seemed to say.

The line starts up again as Rocio picks up her tools, and gradually her hand movements smooth and quicken. She tells her friends.

The next day the BP Mailbox had several ideas, and the following day, more than 20. Francis and Kiely, anxious to build on small

Figure 1.4 Hundreds of Reynosa associate suggestions like this one added up to big productivity gains.

BP Program Associates' Suggestion

What is your **IDEA?**	Name of team or employee	Date _____ *11-19* _____ *BP* _____

At workstation 4, change the manual press to a pneumatic one, and add foam tape

How will it help us?

To work faster

Impact (Genshi)

Supplier:	TRW
Description:	Switch the manual press to a pneumatic one
Name of part:	Hazard Switch
Line:	Honda 63750
Date of implementation:	January 25

Impact:　1. *Cycle time reduced 4.9 seconds*
　　　　　2. *Easier to grab the screwdriver handle*

successes, post 65 ideas from 13 line operators on a tracking chart, and next to each idea the owner's name is clearly written.

Good ideas, however, do not guarantee implementation. It takes support from plant engineering and maintenance to make other changes. The Director of Operations had to be convinced to re-prioritize existing engineering and maintenance time to implement the many suggestions.

Typically, the Honda BPrs want to first select a focus and estab-lish the performance baseline and key measurables against which improvements will be measured. The next step in the process is to analyze the data and ask questions such as "Why is the production efficiency 66 percent?" or "What are the barriers to productivity?" This step prioritizes and focuses ideas and elicits excitement from the production associates.

A synergy develops between production associates who are process experts and the BP engineers, who see improvement oppor-tunities in process and product waste. From the marriage of the idea to the implementation plan, continuous improvements that dra-matically raise productivity are born.

It's Not Engineering—It's Communication

The Reynosa project is not unlike most BP projects. They all hinge on communication—from employees on the line to executives whose real-time support is a basic requirement for success. The simplicity of the concept baffles managers who may be expecting work requiring minimal upper-level commitment—"edicted excellence."

Indeed, the Reynosa project was headed to oblivion as executives, part of the continuing "parade" of plant visitors, attempted to cut short project meetings to board airplanes, leaving plant personnel with ongoing, unidentifiable shortage problems.

Frustration fuels action, and Francis and Kiely challenged management commitment to accountability by calling upstream parts suppliers to a group meeting in Reynosa, where the results of their pareto analysis on parts shortages identified the top four or five offenders. Kiely describes that meeting as chaotic, when hastily-assembled overheads pounded away at waste—rejected parts, unaccounted-for rework, downtime, premium airfreight charges, second inspection costs, etc.—caused by the lack of communication and cooperation.

What better way to illustrate another tenet of the Honda BP philosophy—the 3A's? To understand a problem, go to the *actual spot*, examine the *actual part,* and see the *actual situation.*

TRW supplier management had to learn from actual visits who their internal customer really was—Rocio and her colleagues. Management had to see and experience the pain caused by a failed philosophy that tried to inspect quality into a product. And management had to be held accountable.

Honda BP engineers revolutionized old practice when they marked each improvement suggestion with the originator's name, in the same way they simultaneously marked each parts shortage with the name of the accountable manager.

CELEBRATE THE RESULTS

Change may sometimes be painful, but it is always powerful. With BP, a process limited to a 13-week start-up, the results are powerful and immediate. Reynosa was ripe for change, and the results showed it.

Good pieces produced per man-hour at the beginning of the project measured 4.93 units. After 13 weeks, the number rose to 7.6 pieces, an increase of 54 percent. Line balance improved from 55.5 percent to 72.5 percent; throughput time dropped from 10 minutes, 43 seconds to 9 minutes. Production efficiency, 66 percent at the start, rose to 85 percent, well on the path to excellence. One year into the program, manufacturing associates had generated 432 suggestions, of which 340 were adopted.

But the numbers don't tell the whole story. Honda believes in crediting its accomplishment to the real experts. In the Reynosa experience, the experts who produced incredible gains in less than four months got their due. Rodriguez and his team—many of whom lived in makeshift, temporary housing—worked long hours preparing to take the results of their work public. For most of them, it was the first time they had spoken to a large group; and for all of them, it was the first time they had stood before management. Reynosa and Honda team members' excitement built as they assembled data, drawings, and idea storyboards.

On the day of the presentation, TRW and Honda executives flew in to hear the remarkable story and celebrate the results. Rodriguez and his team presented the results of their BP activity to Honda and TRW executives, many of whom had never seen—and perhaps had not expected—this type of change from a group of production workers. Proud co-workers cheered them on as cameras flashed, and production associates donned new BP Program white smocks modeled after the Honda white uniform.

LESSONS LEARNED

Empowerment, communication, first things first, how to gain management commitment, the 3A's—all of these hard lessons were learned during this early BP project. Andre Gold, former TRW vice

Figure 1.5 TRW's Reynosa plant associates received recognition certificates "for their contribution and participation in the BP Program conducted on the Honda Hazard Switch Line."

president, now president of airbag supplier BAICO in Tennessee, remembers, "We thought it would be difficult to start a project in that multilingual environment, but we learned that BP transcends land and culture boundaries. We listened very carefully to the ideas of associates who know the problems on the lines, and we implemented numerous suggestions," explains Gold. "Many of these ideas yielded only very small benefits, but when taken together, the small changes resulted in dramatic improvements."

> *"BP transcends land and*
> *culture boundaries"*
> —Andre Gold

BP Successes Multiply

Parker Hannifin

Larry Hopcraft, president of the automotive and refrigeration group of Parker Hannifin, cites impressive results from a sampling of 25 BP projects conducted throughout his company. Since 1991, Parker has completed over 250 BP projects. (See Figure 1.7 on page 20.)

The Cleveland, Ohio-based billion-dollar producer makes a variety of fluid and motion control products such as valves, hoses, and pumps. Parker had "been down the road" with quality projects and big-bucks quality initiatives, none of which produced lasting results. Parker is experienced with other supplier improvement programs as well, like GM's PICOS, Ford's 3- to 5-day kaizen events, some of Chrysler's programs, as well as its own earlier quality initiatives. "They are all good," says Hopcraft, "but we learned some important lessons from Honda."

Hopcraft asked one of his managers upon his return from Honda to tell what he had learned. He saved the handwritten answer shown in Figure 1.6, because it summarizes what he would say to other companies considering various improvement techniques.

Lessons spring from values, and, according to Hopcraft, "these were the values our management perceived existed at Honda, and we found them important to improve performance....We all work to those values, and Honda had them."

Russ Coons, Parker Hannifin director of quality, lived through the entire quality improvement process at Parker. Over ten years ago, Parker's chairman, Patrick Parker, had an epiphany. "If," recalls Coons, "the company survived to the year 2000, it would have been by accident." Parker wanted a plan, and he commissioned his vice

Figure 1.6 Important Lessons from Honda

Important Lessons from Honda

Total Understanding of Company Mission and Philosophies

- Customer driven
- Respect for the individual
  - Employee involvement (safety, quality, cost)
  - People oriented
  - Thoughtful, complete orientation activity
- Teamwork
  - Open offices
  - Absence of status symbols
  - Joy of work
- Excellence
- Long-term outlook
- Attention to detail
  - Do the homework

president of manufacturing, along with two other execs, to develop a scenario that would allow top corporate officers attending his midyear planning meeting to address issues that would form the foundation of a plan.

They brainstormed six different issues that all pointed to one critical need—experience. Hopcraft recalls, "We had to use some skills that we hadn't exercised before." They devised a clever rotation scheme that moved key personnel through the completed plant projects. Gradually, Parker associates from different plants had the opportunity to learn and work on these 90-day transformation projects.

Eight steps to success

---

*A mechanism for change at every
level, with every employee*

BP became such an embedded process at Parker that the program acquired a new name, "Targets/BP." Honda is in fact pleased when a supplier takes BP to heart and gives the process a "custom identity and a custom name." At Parker, the title "Targets" stands for Parker's Total Quality Management system to build a Better Parker.

Russ Coons describes Targets/BP as a simple eight-step methodology.

Step 1, Project Planning—Planning guarantees that if associates are going to work intensively for three months, they are addressing the right problem!

Step 2, Process Selection—Covers writing a scope statement that defines in one or two sentences the boundaries of the project. "We found," says Coons, "that projects keep expanding on you, and the only way to maintain focus is to stick to your defined scope statement!"

Step 3, Baseline Data Collection—Expands the metrics that describe a specific projection or location, the baseline against which all results will be measured.

Step 4, Situation Analysis—Coons calls this piece the most crucial part of the transformation, a time when confidence develops between associates and the core team, a time for observing what Honda calls "learning the details." "Remember, your competitors have equal access to materials, machines, buildings, location, so what we are trying to reach is something other than those factors that will make us competitive. It's in the details where you win and lose."

Step 5, Goal Setting—Parker and Honda believe that the team should collectively set goals that must be:

- Easily understood,
- Measurable, and
- Achievable.

Step 6, Implementation—Key to building momentum for the BP initiatives at Parker has been the idea of quick successes. Parker uses quick successes, picking the low-hanging fruit early in the project, to help remove barriers and develop team confidence. Another key to successful implementation recommended by Parker is providing employee coverage for each shift, because this is the point at which process line associates need the most assistance.

Step 7, Baseline Data ("After") Collection—Parker has found that, ideally, the time to capture post-implementation data should be as long as possible. But realistically, time constraints generally limit this phase to two to four weeks.

Step 8, Management Review—Parker's management review allows associates to review their progress as they assemble "before and after" photographs and data that tell the story in their presentation. Parker sends formal invitations from the BP team; the event becomes a learning experience and a celebration.

One more thing...

BP itself is an improving process, and Parker uses a post-project BP survey to monitor the effectiveness, as well as the improvement opportunities, of the process. The survey also evaluates team composition and dynamics, an unusual but honest way to work on the process itself.

Parker takes Targets to the next tier

Having learned and adapted BP, Parker proudly points to the fact that very quickly they took the process to other suppliers. Parker has invited about a dozen next-tier suppliers to send employees to Parker, where they learn the process and see actual results; they then return home to share the lessons and techniques with fellow employees. Hopcraft believes, "It's always a good experience, every time we do it...no question that the education one gets is valuable."

A warning from one "who has been there"

Hopcraft knows that everyone is "enamored by the results we talked about initially here. Everyone would like to do this, and they want to do it fast." What could be wrong with that eagerness, you might ask. "They aren't willing to commit the people. You see," Hopcraft says, emphasizing the word *value*, "the value of BP is not the savings—it's a tool to change your culture to those important lessons learned from Honda....If you do it just for results, to get 40 percent improvement in productivity, for example, then it won't be different from any other programs. But if you use it to change culture, that's where the real value is." Hopcraft believes, and Parker is proving, that companies can progress faster and faster, the more responsive and prepared the culture is for lean manufacturing.

Figure 1.7   Parker Hannifin Targets/BP Results

Parker Hannifin Targets/BP Results, Average of 25 Projects

Expenditures	$15K (not including cost of associates)		
Savings	$107K		
Throughput	Before	After	Improvement
WIP ($)	29,184	784	98%
Time (hr)	65	7	89%
Distance (ft)	733	141	81%
Productivity:			
Area (sq. ft)	1,794	1,078	40%
Output (pieces/hr)	61	89	46%

Copyright Parker Hannifin. Reprinted with permission.

Donnelly Corporation

Donnelly Corporation of Holland, Michigan, previously family-owned, now a public company, has been included in *The 100 Best Companies to Work for in America* compiled by Robert Levering and Milton Moskowitz (New York: Doubleday, 1993). But about eight years ago this producer of most of the mirrors shipped to worldwide auto producers was less than happy with its quality performance.

Honda recommended that Donnelly try a BP project, and sent several Marysville, Ohio, associates including Chuck Richardson, and Shige Nakazato to teach BP. Seven years and over 200 projects later, Donnelly Corporate Director of Quality Systems Jim Cleveland is convinced that BP will take the company into the single-digit quality levels they want. Previous quality improvement initiatives had not been conducted company-wide, nor had they been standardized, and Cleveland feels that being decentralized slowed them down.

Typical results for Donnelly continuous improvement include 30 percent productivity gains, 60 percent reduced floor space, 90 percent in-process inventory reduction, and 30 percent scrap reduction. The company has stopped calling their program BP as it has been absorbed into the Donnelly culture.

The paint shop

Paint shops continue to be challenges to all manufacturing quality experts, and Donnelly was no different. One approach is robotics and sequenced paint scheduling. Honda, however, advised the company to study the paint shop *before* they automated it. Moving to higher volumes without fixing some basic problems would have been a mistake, they advised, and the Honda recommendation was to learn good techniques in a small area and then transfer those gains into the larger automated paint area. BP experts feared that

Donnelly might transfer bad habits into the new area. So Donnelly took a break to gather actual information from existing operation times, scrap levels, product workflow, layout, inventory levels, efficiencies, downtimes—"All," remembers Cleveland, "the things that describe manufacturing."

The results were convincing, and so Donnelly moved on to other BP challenges, one of which was interior mirrors for the Accord and the Civic. Again, results more than supported the effort, as productivity improved over 20 percent and in process dropped 80 to 90 percent.

Cleveland cites the need for direct active support from all levels, "not just a passive 'okay, go ahead, we'll see you later' type of support. BP techniques are most effective when everybody in the organization understands what BP is, how it is used, and the expected gains. If you don't start with very broad active support, you may have small areas with good results, but it won't last, because as the champions move on, key measures won't be in place at the corporate level to drive lasting change." Cleveland cites that one of the things that was most difficult for Donnelly, a very democratically organized company was to become organized from the top of the organization down.

A second mistake Cleveland cites in their approach to BP was that sometimes "we use more sophisticated tools than we really need." Start simple, and remember that you can always add more sophisticated tools later, "but you can take 50 percent of the savings from an idea by using simple tools."

Over 1,000, or about 70 percent, of Donnelly's employees have been touched by the BP experience, 30 percent directly. The next big challenge is customer ppm of 10 by the year 2002. One smaller Donnelly plant in Holland, Michigan, producing interior trim and interior lights, has already achieved 50 ppm; Grand Haven is at approximately 100 ppm. The company boasts of much transfer of BP from one plant to another.

Cleveland sees more work ahead of him, however. "We have made huge progress over the years.... The secret is standardization and consistency.... It is clear to me that BP is the genesis of what we are doing now."

The Progressive Stamping Success Story

Progressive Industries started out over 40 years ago as a die maker, but soon the company moved into making actual stampings. In 1986, the company teamed up with Honda, after being selected with 6 others from a field of over 100 stampers, as HAM's first stamping suppliers. As Progressive grew its capabilities, so grew Honda's trust. Progressive started to perform welding and assembly and began consulting on better ways to build dies.

The two companies' employment policies seemed to mesh well, and Progressive became a target for BP activities. Ruston Simon, president and CEO, remembers that during the time another stamping supplier was experiencing performance problems, Honda assigned a group to camp out at the plant, and he was impressed. Although Progressive was not the first BP project for Honda's supply base, when Progressive "got wind of it," says Simon, "we raised our hand. We requested that they consider a BP activity in our plant because we knew we would be growing, and we wanted to take advantage of this new technique. We didn't know exactly what we were asking for, but we trusted them. We didn't think they would take advantage of us."

Like many proponents, Simon was more interested in perfecting his processes. "We didn't go into it because we were looking for cost savings. We wanted to make ourselves better." And the results were not long in coming, as BP teams worked on documentation, setups, visibility management, and other floor issues.

Taking off the blinders

"We took one machine and used it as a laboratory, and then we took it to other machines." But not all of this change was fun, however. Skilled tradespeople on the floor—tool-and-die makers—tended to be suspicious at first, as was production floor management; people newer to the company took the changes easier.

As a growing company, Progressive had the advantage of reinventing itself as it grew. Simon used tapes and training, as well as the visible commitment of two full-time Honda associates on site, to persuade the holdouts. Projects included visual management improvements, some ergonomic changes that smoothed operators' jobs, housekeeping fixes (tools), and other simple ideas that tallied up to big productivity changes.

The automotive business will either polish you or grind you down, and Progressive learned the advantage of having one more powerful tool in its toolbox. Simon feels that Honda's game plan of assembling less and less on the assembly line and relying more on its suppliers to ship in more integrated modules, has been facilitated by suppliers like Progressive maturing its process capabilities through BP. Assembling the auto body, for example, has changed. The frame requires more process maturity of suppliers because it contains larger subassemblies, which means less welding, a faster assembly process, and higher quality of pretested and prechecked assemblies direct shipped.

The other implication for suppliers of the move to preassembly of bigger component assemblies is more business for the second tier. Certainly developing a world-class assembly supplier entails less risk in-house and offers more flexibility than investing in another assembly line. Simon believes that this is one more reason why "my business is shifting" and one more reason for suppliers to tackle BP.

Real benefits accrued to Progressive as improvements were moved to other machine centers. A long list of small improvements added up to significant changes for Progressive. Setup times dropped from one hour to thirty minutes. Tool maintenance was streamlined; small tool holder compartments were attached to the press. Many changes simply made associates' work easier and more manageable, as in the Reynosa plant story.

"I only wish we had done as good a job with our supplier as our customer has done with us," Simon concludes.

GM has PICOS, Ford has Q1, Solectron has its Customer Satisfaction Index. The list of corporate quality improvement programs grows. Honda's approach, its BP program, targets five strategic improvement areas:

1. Best Position—improve global competitiveness;

2. Best Productivity—improve the process;

3. Best Product—improve quality and delivery;

4. Best Price—decrease cost; and

5. Best Partners—improve Honda/supplier relationship.

Honda, like all automotive producers, needs world-class suppliers. Management recognizes the company's dependence on a network of special partners, not all of whose 400 members are located within 24 hours of assembly plants. It's not enough for a supplier to have periodically demonstrated superior quality and delivery, along with reasonable costs. Consistency takes commitment, and Honda looks to its BP program to help suppliers build internal excellence and participate in the company's challenge to improve its competitive position in the world-class market.

Reynosa associates took BP and matured with it, and they are still doing extremely well. In 1996, the plant received an award for being TRW's most improved plant. Improvements gained through the BP activities benefit competitors' lines as well; results over all lines show lasting and comprehensive change.

On the pioneering Reynosa project, 53 out of 65 ideas were implemented. The balance were duplicates, not feasible, or saved for later applications. Regardless of their "disposition," an associate

Figure 1.8 BP Results, Reynosa — 23 lines, over 4 departments

Operator headcount   25.24% reduction, per project.
(Honda policy requires no layoffs due to displacement of operators.)

BP plant-wide involvement   88.68% of all employees, over
                                all lines

Suggestions received for 11 months

1996 year-to-date   1614 ideas, or 10 per associate

Average daily production rate   15.24% increase per project

Cycle time reduction   19.19% per project

Average waste cost reduction   82.11% per project

Average downtime reduction   54.15% per project

name was attached to every one. As ideas were tracked, associates were kept informed of the status of their contributions.

"Let the data lead you." —Dorian Shainin

Shewhart Award winner and quality guru Dorian Shainin taught that the truth lies in the data. BP experts understand that one never knows where the BP process will take improvement teams, but the communication and data analysis and data gathering steps will, even without dedicated execution, identify major improvement opportunities. The rest is up to you.

Figure 1.9 BP Expert Suggestions Mean Big Productivity Improvements

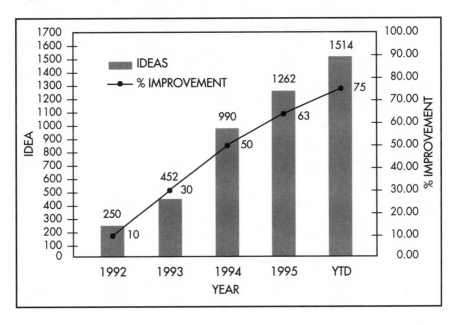

Figure 1.10 BP Phase 1 Results

BP Phase 1 Results

- 70 Suppliers
- 118 Projects
- 48% Productivity increase
- 7.25% Cost improvement

2

Terry Maruo, the Father of BP

Lessons from the Great Sensei

THE GREAT SENSEI ON LEADERSHIP

*Being a leader is very difficult. The leader has
to have teaching abilities. If he is not able to
teach the leaders of his team, they are not going
to be able to trust him. The leader needs to have
confidence in evaluating members of his team,
and he needs to provide them with direction.*

*It is dangerous for the commander to give his
subordinates the command, "At ease," because
that leaves them to do whatever they like.*

*It is not enough to support the associates.
Make sure they know that the enemy is to
their right. Be at ease with caution. You will
lose your ability to fight if you are at ease,
if you let your guard down.*

If you are comfortable, you lose your alertness.

*Small challenges, small successes, raise the bar;
small challenges, bigger successes, raise the bar.*

—Teruyuki Maruo

Teruyuki (Terry) Maruo, the father of BP, learned many valuable lessons from Soichiro Honda, and in all those lessons, the word *gemba* most defines the continuous improvement philosophy that Mr. Honda lived and taught his associates and suppliers. *Gemba*—the actual place, *gembitsu*, the actual part, and *gengitsu*, the actual situation—guided all of Mr. Honda's work life.

THE ROOTS OF BP

"We call it *nariuki*—a natural process—it just happens. We learned that by improving the manufacturing process, we would improve quality. Forty years ago in Japan, we saw quality stagnating; and because of Japan's lack of natural resources, we believe that it is each person's responsibility to make the most of the resources we have," explains Maruo. Japanese producers have learned to make the most of their opportunities.

Maruo created the Honda BP approach in Japan over 20 years ago from the teachings of Mr. Honda and from his own 15 years' quality experience, along with his belief that teamwork and hands-on

Figure 2.1 Teruyuki Maruo, born October 16, 1943. Currently resides in the United Kingdom, where he is spreading the BP message to European suppliers.

learning have the power to make important changes in the way people work. "My goal in 1976 was to fortify the ranks of the suppliers to achieve cost-down activities." Maruo took his powerful methodology to the United States in 1979 and later to England and Canada.

Even before 1976, from his position in quality management, Maruo and his people spent most of their time in suppliers' plants. "Our goal in the quality department was to go to the *gemba* where we always discovered material waste. What started as a quality issue—poor quality, many rejects, much material thrown out—proved that the actual production process itself was not good."

Maruo's first opportunity for change appeared in material usage, especially stamping. Stamping operations frequently cut parts from the middle of a steel coil, creating 50 percent material as waste.

"When we changed our style of stamping, we were able to cut waste down to 20 percent and we increased our material usage by 20 to 30 percent. With coils, for example, we had been wasting almost half of our material in the process. In Japan, where resources are scarce, this was considered even more of a waste. That was what got me started in BP activities." Maruo realized that even greater potential lay with U.S. producers who had in the fat 60s forgotten the lessons that they had shared 20 years earlier with Japan.

Figure 2.2   Stamping process before BP and after Redesign.

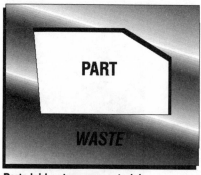

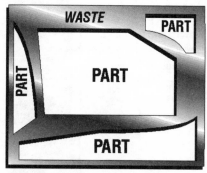

Parts laid out on raw material, showing enormous waste

Stamping parts' sequence redesigned to maximize use of full coil, minimize scrap

INVEST THE TIME

How long does it take to show significant results? BP's basic time line requires 3 months, or 13 weeks, to get going. Maruo believes that "if you have seen no changes after three months, it is not going to work. Within three months, you should see results—restructured lines, efficiency improvement—in *gemba*." If not, it's time to move on.

"Remember, we are trying to do *knowledge change*. Most changes start to take place in four to five weeks. Here you start to develop good ideas." If companies are not starting to make some progress after a month or so, probably their management is not committed, and they do not understand. "However, if they do not understand in three months, they probably are not going to be successful, so do not waste your time."

Maruo came to understand firsthand the power of focused kaizen activities, especially in basic operations such as stamping and component assembly. "Usually in a stamping line, in one month you will see results. If you don't, that company doesn't have the incentive."

THREE PATHS TO IMPROVEMENT

There are three ways to improve a supplier's productivity and its cost structure:

1. The Lopez (named after GM's heavy-handed former head of purchasing)—a hit-them-over-the-head approach which makes them go broke and forces the customer to change suppliers;

2. The BP approach to improved *productivity* and *efficiency;* and

3. The BP *material* utilization techniques.

Fortify the Supplier

When Maruo first arrived in the United States, he saw most "supplier improvement" techniques falling into Method #1, the Lopez approach: "My approach was to focus on teamwork in smaller companies. I realized the importance of fortifying the team, strengthening their capability, working with them, making them a strong organization." So his first goal—the *real* goal—became the challenge of helping suppliers to become strong. "We knew if we could make them stronger, they would continue to improve—on their own."

Do not confuse Honda BP with cost-down approaches. Honda shares each supplier improvement that generates cost savings 50/50 with suppliers. The first objective is perfecting the process. Good quality and delivery performance will naturally flow from a smooth process.

Doing It the Hard Way

BP practitioners have come to expect major scrap reductions, quality improvements, and productivity gains. "We knew from Japan that we would get major results in manpower improvement, material yield, material utilization—all major factors in suppliers' cost structures."

What if suppliers are slow to respond? When necessary, Maruo escalates directly to management, especially in companies with unions. The point is "trust" in the no layoff policy of BP. Take a very careful approach, he advises, so that the end result is not perceived as more work for the employees.

Moreover, Maruo recommends working very closely with top management, right from the beginning, especially if productivity gains result in "excess workers." BP experts emphasize the importance of their rule guaranteeing employees' jobs: If a job is eliminated because of improvement activity, workers are not displaced. Innovative solutions to excess head counts and capacity include, for example, reviewing overtime that goes directly to the bottom line. Transfer or retrain and redeploy associates, but do not lay them off because of BP successes!

BP experts try to lead American companies into a broader perspective. Many very successful BP projects have been conducted in union shops, but union environments require that special attention be paid in the planning stage to worker issues.

LEARNING TO SEE

"Gemba is a gold mine."

Terry Maruo

Sometimes the layout of a process, sometimes the operator, sometimes the equipment cause productivity losses. Maruo looks at all of these factors, but he remembers learning from Mr. Honda that environmental conditions make a big difference. "We noticed that in unairconditioned facilities, where it was very hot, we always saw poor-quality parts, and in those areas we replaced those workers with robots. If it was too hot or too cold, or if there was too much noise, or if the environment was not friendly to human productivity—difficult, dangerous, or dirty—we would replace human workers with robots."

Co-author Rick Mayo learned Maruo's lessons well in the five senses—hearing, smell, sight, touch, and taste. With each plant tour, Mauro stopped to ask, "What do you see? What do you hear?" And if his student answered, "I smell smoke, I hear noises in the equipment," the great sensei would point out all the things the student had missed. "He taught me how to look beyond, to look deeper, to focus on what you really see."

Ask yourself, for example, if that CNC machine is working, or if it is waiting for a person, or if the operator is waiting for the machine. Evaluate the lighting: How clean are the bulbs? Since many operators must look at small parts for long hours, you must understand how well they can see their work.

Question how hard associates are working, because working hard does not mean working smart. "Remember as you observe the lines, much activity does not necessarily mean a good plant." Maruo

---

Lessons in Using the Five Senses from the Great Sensei

Hearing. Stamping machines make a rhythmic "ka-chunk, ka-chunk" when they are running well. If they aren't making noise, you aren't making money.

Smell. In Honda's Anna, Ohio, engine plant, which houses a state-of-the-art aluminum foundry, there are no toxic smells. The plant has the smell of a laboratory.

Sight. A well-run operation has few ripples on the water; products move downstream through operations seemingly effortlessly.

Touch. If a machine is hot or greasy to the human touch, or if it feels dirty, as if periodic maintenance were long forgotten, you can expect the rest of the process and the products to be the same—worn, dirty, and difficult to work with.

Taste. Does the air leave a toxic taste in your mouth?

urged his students to use their five senses from the moment they stepped into a plant. If you smell a toxic odor, for example, check for the root cause. Maruo taught his BP pioneers to focus immediately on these environmental issues, because they had everything to do with the safety and quality of work life.

MORE LESSONS FROM THE GREAT SENSEI

Maruo taught his students how to walk into any supplier, in any situation, with any problem, and solve it. He taught his students how, in less than 15 minutes and using all 5 senses, to understand how a plant works, whether machines are going well, and where the problems are.

Trust

"Suppliers don't trust purchasing, because purchasing means cost, but," taught Maruo, "*they must trust you.* Suppliers must develop confidence in you. Suppliers may not trust purchasing, but you want them to trust you." Maruo was challenged from his first day in the United States to change that perception, and 400 Honda suppliers speak to the success of his work.

Traditional purchasing practices position purchasing and suppliers in the cost arena. But, said the great sensei, "If suppliers trust you, they will follow you."

How to Start the Process—Don't Just Do It!

Planning is 90 percent of the business of continuous improvement. One of Maruo's experiential teachings was that even before a team is formed, even before the numbers are collected, BP requires planning. Remembers one of his students, "When we came back (from seeing Japanese plants), even before we started our BP program, Terry forced us to develop a plan for continuous improvement. It took six months!"

What Maruo wanted was an *image,* and he needed to know that his followers saw the same image in their mind's eye. Objectively, that image can be broken into dozens of pictels, each representing one important piece of the whole picture. Planners were forced to answer questions such as what is the approach, how many people will you need, and what kinds of people, what skills will they need, what skills do they already have. Nailing down each valuable element of the image, Maruo asked BP pioneers to describe what they were going to do on arrival at the supplier's plant, what they planned to do on the first day, the second day, the third day, and so on.

Students developed BP plans in great detail, but they still were allowed—perhaps expected—to make judgment errors. "Our first BP project we focused on costs, and he let us do that, and within days we figured out we were on the wrong path—ourselves," remembers an early team member.

Later, Maruo reminded the team of the primary goal—to help suppliers become more competitive and more self-reliant: "If you focus on improvement and making things better, the result is merit—merit is an improvement that affects cost but that may not be cost down."

For example, if the supplier quotes scrap in raw material as his biggest problem, don't rearrange the line, because the quickest way to improve productivity is to improve quality by reducing scrap, rework, and rejects. What remains is product integrity.

---

*"Take out scrap, rework, and rejects, and
what remains is product integrity."*

Terry Maruo

Each time a questionable part travels down the line, where an associate spots it and takes it off, touches it, fixes and reassembles it, there is a "double whammy"; the company has lost the opportunity—forever—to sell a good part, and the original opportunity to make a good part.

The Great Sensei on Winning and Teamwork

The magic is…there is no magic!

Rick Mayo, student of Terry Maruo

BP simplifies. BP attacks complexity and removes layers of systems and management plans to reveal the heart of a healthy, empowered, and lean manufacturing process. Like Soichiro Honda, Terry Maruo and all BP experts understand the dynamics of The Race. Mr. Honda said, "Winning is everything. Second place is never honored or remembered," and BP is a valuable advantage. "We are all

Figure 2.3 Life is a Race—Be sure everyone gets a fair shot. "At the beginning of the race, everyone starts on the same line. But focus, determination, and speed, supported by the pit crew's teamwork, determine positions at the finish line."

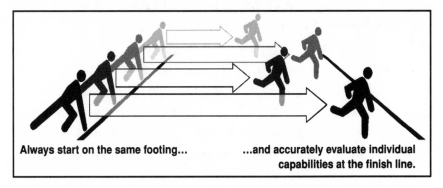

Always start on the same footing...   ...and accurately evaluate individual capabilities at the finish line.

given the same opportunity to start and finish the race, but the finish line shows the actual result."

At the track, people are always being judged. "Sometimes," warns Maruo, "life or the judges show favoritism. If there is favoritism, people know not to trust the race."

❀

THE GREAT SENSEI ON TEAMWORK

Indy car drivers know that they themselves do not individually win the race. Hundreds of other professionals—from the pit crew all the way back to the engine designers—determine who gets the trophy long before the flag drops. Be sure, for teamwork's sake, that all suppliers start out on the same footing. What happens next is natural competition.

What makes the winning difference is people. Pit crews make the difference, each with different skills and training—the engine designer, the wheel man, the timer, the parts jockey.

According to Maruo, "A team is not successful unless it has people that have different ideas. I don't need someone that thinks just like I do. If you have everyone thinking the same way, you will have a lot of yes men, and no progress. I purposefully gather people that have different ideas. For example, Tom Kiely, Rick Mayo, and Mike Goddard [original BP team members] are very different people, and that's what makes them a very strong team."

Maruo believes in the magical number seven. When he started BP in Japan, all his teams started with seven people. "People cannot operate alone. They need to work in teams. It's a natural human weakness." Look for seven people who have strong technical skills and personal communication skills, but who are not well-rounded. "I like

Figure 2.4 Build the team with 7 complementary individuals.

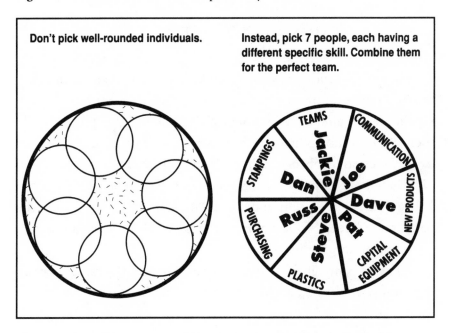

Don't pick well-rounded individuals.

Instead, pick 7 people, each having a different specific skill. Combine them for the perfect team.

to work with people that are not yet well-rounded, geometrically more triangular."

One team member may be very good at die maintenance, and one may be good at controlling material waste, while number three is good at process change....Gathered together on a team, they become a whole unit. "It's better to have seven partially complete people than to have one complete, well-rounded person. One person is not enough."

Pick a strong manager and leaders that will take into consideration other people, their attitudes, their skills. "The best leaders are hard workers and strong pushers, but they must have compassion as well."

One of Maruo's best students is not good at everything, and if he were good at everything, he would not be a good manager, "but I do admire his confidence, and I have faith that he will work with my ideas."

RAISING THE BAR, ENDLESSLY

One of Maruo's most effective teaching images is "Raising the Bar" because when he picks team members of various complementary capabilities, he already knows their strength. How they use and build their strength and agility determines their position at the finish line. Typical Maruo feedback might be (pointing to each team member): "My judgment is that *you* are number one; *you* are number five, but I would like to see *you* number one." Maruo was always raising the bar. "It was," recalls one willing victim, "endless. Terry did a very good job of keeping us on our toes."

"That was my goal," answers Maruo. "If I set the target way up high, they would be overwhelmed. It would be too far. Always set the bar just a *little bit* higher."

The process of raising the bar, making more changes, and repeating the process, calls for much self-evaluation. Original BP team members recall spending hours not discussing their wins, but trying to understand what went wrong, because, "to improve our weak

Figure 2.5   Raising the Bar

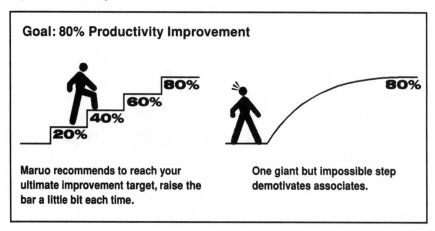

Goal: 80% Productivity Improvement

20% 40% 60% 80%

80%

Maruo recommends to reach your
ultimate improvement target, raise the
bar a little bit each time.

One giant but impossible step
demotivates associates.

points, we didn't focus on our strengths, we focused on our weaknesses." Carried further into daily BP operations, managers deliberately plan to let associates feel good about their achievement very quickly. "Monthly targets and monthly reviews allowed us to feel good for about a week," remembers co-author Rick Mayo, "but he wouldn't let us feel good for very long. We stayed focused that way."

THE GREAT SENSEI'S PERSONAL RACE

The automotive industry will continue to be a fight between Goliaths attempting to crush opponents with their size, and Davids, agile, smaller, smarter competitors who find a way to be in too many spots in the arena to be cornered. Good competitors raise the bar, and they never are at ease.

"We are," says Maruo, "always thinking of Toyota. Every time. Every time.... They need BP activities and they have started a kaizen center in Cincinnati. They need BP activities. *They like our kaizen.*" Maruo is not worried about other competitors. Toyota's strength and financial comfort power are always at the back of his head, just beyond his seeing or hearing, but "They are always here. This is my race. My race."

3

The Global Gospel According to Honda

INTRODUCTION

Honda is one of the leading global organizations today with 130 production facilities in 52 countries supplying Honda products to most countries of the world. This relatively young company approaches its global mission through integrating the company's philosophy, organization structure, a strategy of self-reliance, and its new "Strategy for the Americas." These form the foundation for the company's dramatic growth worldwide.

The strategy for continued global success that will take Honda into the 21st century can be summarized in three steps:

1. Stay close to customers.

2. Understand their needs.

3. Exceed their expectations.

"Originally, Honda was a small local company in Hamamatsu producing motorcycles," remembers Takeo Fukui, President and CEO of Honda of America Manufacturing, "but Mr. Honda had an international viewpoint. In 1956, he developed a philosophy of becoming an international and global company. He moved the company headquarters to Tokyo, an international industry center." Other well-considered steps took Honda further into the international scene. In 1954, even as the company faced a financial crisis, President Honda reinforced his global vision for Honda technology—"Since technology knows no national boundaries, we must always keep our eyes open to the entire world."[1]

In 1996, Mr. Fukui became President of Honda of America, succeeding Takeshi Yamada, who moved up as HAM's Chairman. Fukui assumed this leadership role for HAM at a time of innovation for the North American auto/motorcycle complex, when many unique

Figure 3.1 Worldwide Operations

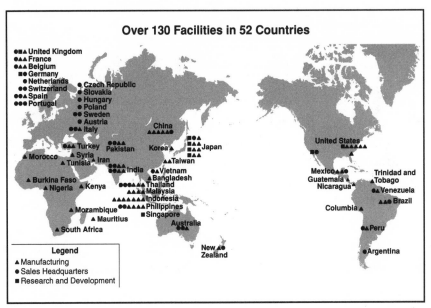

models were launched. Within the company's overall expansion plan, more production and design, more models, and more suppliers would fill the growth plans. The Honda organization worldwide sold over 7,260,000 motorcycles and autos in 1996, and 2,383,000 power products; sales and revenues increased 7.2 percent from the previous year, an increase primarily attributed to higher car sales in Japan and increased motorcycle and power products sales in overseas markets.

In the United States alone, Honda has captured the top position in the individual, non-fleet four-door sedan market. The suppliers' role in Honda's extended enterprise can only continue to grow—in their size, in their technology contributions, and in their pursuit of BP's powerful improvement solutions.

Coming from Honda Motor Co. in Japan, Fukui's career at Honda has included senior positions in research and development, and president of Honda Racing Corporation. "I had many communications with Mr. Honda that helped me understand the racing spirit. When we face a challenging problem that we must

Figure 3.2 Honda U.S. Exports on the Rise

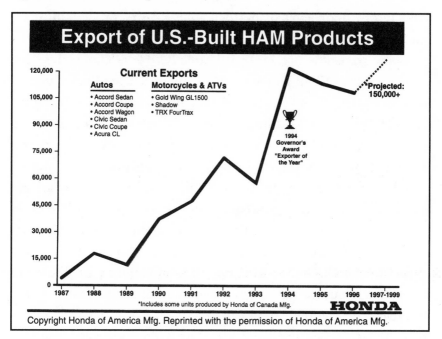

Copyright Honda of America Mfg. Reprinted with the permission of Honda of America Mfg.

overcome, then we experience the racing spirit.... Racing itself is a global activity that goes beyond culture."

Fukui believes that Honda will continue to meet the challenge of being global. "To be global, or international, means understanding and going beyond culture. You have to respect the other country's culture, introduce the Honda culture, and work to create a new Honda Way."

BP Drives Honda GlobalEnterprise Growth— A Direct Line into the Future

Further, Fukui sees that "the difference between cultures is not so much what should be done, but how it should be accomplished. In the Honda Way, every activity of the company should focus on the customer." And BP is key to bringing Honda's entire global enterprise into a high level of performance. "Every process must be improved—output, efficiency...."

Fukui traces the origins of BP directly to Mr. Kume, president during the 80s. When Kume assumed the presidency, he wanted to internally strengthen "efficiency," which also translates to productivity. His goal was 3X improvement. "We always had impossible goals. It was like Mission Impossible," recalls Fukui. "That's the Racing Spirit. Now TQM [Total Quality Management] asks us to set achievable [measurable] goals. Kume used apparently unattainable goals to drive big improvements in a short time, and BP became key to achieving internally what was later taken to the supply base.

In November of 1996, Honda of America hosted its first NH (New Honda) Circles World Convention in Columbus, Ohio—the first one held outside Japan. Two hundred seventy-nine circle members selected as winners represented 58 circles from 16 countries—most for the first time—and were treated to speeches, awards, networking, a look at Honda's future, and a trip to the Rock and Roll Hall of Fame in Cleveland.

Honda Motor Co. president Nobuhiko Kawamoto recognized their valued contributions and commitment through which, "from the beginning of product development, Honda of America has become a major manufacturing company in America." He credited their devotion to teamwork and quality with significant growth and improvement, and he predicted that in the year 1996 alone, more than 100,000 associates from Honda and its affiliates would participate in 12,000 NH quality circles around the world.

Honda of America began motorcycle production in 1979 with only 64 associates, but almost ten years later there were four manufacturing plants, Honda Engineering North America, Honda R & D North America, and a major parts distribution facility in Troy, Ohio. Investment in HAM reached $3.5 billion in 1997; the company exports 20 percent of its auto production from its Ohio assembly

Figure 3.3   Growth of Ohio Investment

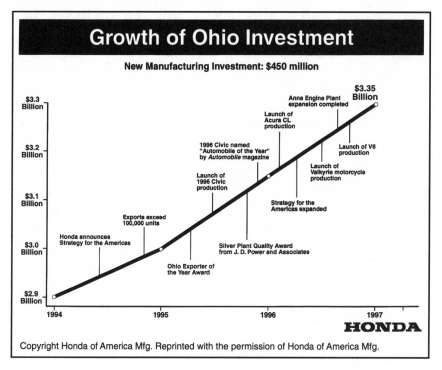

Growth of Ohio Investment

New Manufacturing Investment: $450 million

$3.3 Billion

$3.2 Billion

$3.1 Billion

$3.0 Billion

$2.9 Billion

$3.35 Billion

Anna Engine Plant expansion completed

Launch of Acura CL production

1996 Civic named "Automobile of the Year" by *Automobile* magazine

Launch of V6 production

Launch of Valkyrie motorcycle production

Launch of 1996 Civic production

Exports exceed 100,000 units

Strategy for the Americas expanded

Honda announces Strategy for the Americas

Silver Plant Quality Award from J. D. Power and Associates

Ohio Exporter of the Year Award

1994   1995   1996   1997

HONDA

Copyright Honda of America Mfg. Reprinted with the permission of Honda of America Mfg.

plants. By growing its workforce from 64 to 13,000 associates, Honda of America has matured its product design and production and support capabilities to compete globally.

GROWTH = SPEED, QUALITY, COST

The company's incredible growth story stands in sharp contrast to other industry giants' failure to adapt and move quickly. Dave Nelson started his career at Ross Gear and Tools Co. in Lafayette, Indiana, as a metallurgical technician, later as a quality control manager. Ross manufactured manual and power-steering gears for large trucks. Although the company held 96 percent of its market, when

Nelson and some engineers brainstormed a new product, "it would take years and years to bring out the new gear. We had the best people in the industry. We were recognized as the Cadillac—that's why we held 96 percent of the market—but it took years to design things."

In the automotive industry, new product introductions—speed, as well as quality and cost—will continue to carry the winners over the finish line. Typically, every four years Honda has introduced a full model change for each car: new design, new technology, and new components. Obviously, this cannot happen with a reactive, immature supply base. Honda has many suppliers who make some extraordinarily high technical contributions, and because of them the company was able to move to America, build a new plant, hire new people, and actually create a company and start production generally in less than 2 years from the first shovel of dirt to the building of highly technical and sophisticated parts.

THE COMPANY PRINCIPLE CREATES FIVE UNIFYING PHILOSOPHIES

As a philosophy-driven organization, Honda relies on a handful of very powerful goals and unifying structures to keep its global extended enterprise (plants, suppliers, associates) aligned. These five integrating principles link day-to-day operating decisions on the production floor, in the purchasing and supplier offices, and even in engineering and research and development.

Five integrators link the Honda global extended enterprise:

1. One global philosophy
2. Employee dedication and focus

3. Complementary supply—Each region may support other regions in a global network of complementary supply.

4. Self-reliance

5. Strategy for the Americas

All Honda associates understand and follow the same operating philosophy and principles; they use the same approach to problem-solving and total quality, the facts can be shared globally, and Kawamoto (the current president) believes they "go beyond language and culture. By sharing a problem or objectives among associates, for example, they can recognize the same facts and solve the problems with teamwork."

Susan Insley, HAM's former senior vice president and Anna Engine Plant manager, marks a turning point for Honda and its American facilities in the early 90s. "In 1991, the market was changing. Japan's bubble economy burst, and I think Mr. Kawamoto felt that decision-making took too long, that the company was not using its assets as wisely as it should have—in Japan and around the world. Kawamoto felt he had to change the company, so he went to Mr. Honda, saying, 'I apologize to you, but I am going to have to tear down some things, and then we will rebuild the company.'"

WHEN THE BUBBLE ECONOMY BURST

The following years—1993, 1994, and 1995—were very tough times for Honda. During the Gulf War, people stopped buying cars, and the economy in Japan fractured and tumbled with a terrible deflation. Money had been flowing freely as Japanese investors bought up land, golf courses, and off-shore real estate. When the house of cards crumbled, land prices dropped, and prized real estate was sold with millions of dollars lost. Businesses, large and small, suffered as well.

In the depths of the 1991 recession, many auto producers were struggling; Mazda and Nissan were being watched very closely by the Japanese banks. "In fact," Insley recalls, "in 1995, some news reports speculated on the idea 'wouldn't it be nice if Honda and Mitsubishi would merge?'"

❀

IF YOU BUILD IT, WILL THEY COME?

The automotive industry plays a high-stakes capacity game, a game of corporate chicken with five cars for every four buyers. Each competitor built plants and filled them with equipment and materials in anticipation that demand would materialize. And for some producers, it did, such as for Taurus, the sport-utility vehicles, minivans, and the Accord. Nissan had two wonderful new plants and excess capacity. But closing a plant, especially a new one, in anticipation of unrealized demand, is not part of the game.

Insley's analysis of the crisis and its economic fallout hinges on the capacity and resource utilization issues—"…it became just as cost effective to import cars into Japan and it was consistent with Honda's global business strategy." Kawamoto had some big decisions to make. He withdrew the company from Formula I racing, a very expensive activity, and redirected company energies to the fundamentals of the business. Certain Formula I engineers, some of the finest engineers in the world, were assigned to the new V-6 engine project. Working under accelerated time schedules set by Honda's top management, Japanese R & D engineers, and Honda Purchasing and Quality divisions in concert with American suppliers, met the schedule by completing a new engine whose concept defined the new standard of excellence in engine development.

Kawamoto knew that to play the capacity game he had to do more with the plants operating in America. "Those plants needed to improve productivity and efficiency."

GO TO THE SPOT

In August of 1995, Kawamoto flew to the United States for the launch of the '96 Civic; he used that opportunity to reiterate the company principle—"... to supply products of the highest efficiency at a reasonable price." He stressed the need to supply Honda customers with products that provided quality and value. He also asked managers to achieve cost savings. Managers were asked to study every one of their lines, looking for opportunities. Insley recalls, "Anna had 26 lines, and the onus was on the plant managers to thoroughly understand each line. We did a detailed analysis of existing lines, and with no new investment, we identified bottleneck points and places where we knew we could improve efficiency of the operations. And we would not do it on the backs of the people."

FUTURE GROWTH

BP, already fully deployed, proved to be the most powerful tool in the campaign to supplement Honda suppliers' high-energy associates with a systematic approach.

For example, the Anna engine assembly line was running at 2,100 units per day. "Our target was to achieve about a 10% increase in output. We already produced on three shifts, and we had to get to yet a higher level," remembers Insley. "One of the many solutions we (managers and associates alike) developed was to reduce in-process inventory. We also looked at machine downtime, and setup time reduction. We prepared root cause analysis and developed permanent countermeasures. These changes helped us achieve our target and, of course, improved operations."

Better use of available resources includes power and equipment usage. The Marysville Auto plant's team was planning on taking power costs down by 2 percent to 3 percent, but in some areas the result hit 30 percent. Associates reviewed every single power element—production and nonproduction. In the maintenance area, for example, an associate noticed, as he walked through the plant at a quiet time, the soft hissing of air guns indicating leaks in the air hoses—another waste of energy and resources.

Hundreds of small improvements yielded significant progress toward Kawamoto's edict of doing more with existing resources. And they all reinforced the Honda BP 3A's "Go to the Spot" philosophy.

In 1993, 1994 and 1995, Kawamoto continued to emphasize quality and value goals. BP, already fully deployed, proved to be the most powerful tool in the campaign to supplement Honda suppliers' high-energy associates with a systematic approach. BP speaks from hard data and prioritizes improvement opportunities, the only effective way to improve quality and value. In the midst of these ongoing crusades, purchasing continued to take a high-profile position. "Purchasing," says Insley, "has always been ahead of the manufacturing side at looking for ways to knock out non-value added. I remember BP at purchasing being discussed before TQM was discussed for the company."

Purchasing in the Catbird Seat

Kawamoto believed that he could affect 1994 and 1998 model designs, but it meant doing R & D diffferently, with more supplier and purchasing up-front involvement. "Purchasing," says Insley, "was in the catbird seat, in its growing role with Honda R & D and its intensive work with suppliers."

Eighty percent of the cost of a vehicle comes from parts purchased from someone else. No stronger number is needed to support the Honda philosophy. Purchasing has the constant struggle of balancing the two tensions of highest efficiency and reasonable price.

After Kawamoto divided the company into four regions, the Ohio complex adopted its own brand of TQM with a vengeance. TQM for Honda at that time was very different from what other producers think of when they use the term. "We select a fairly narrow band of what we call TQM. Although many people think of TQM as a result, it is, in fact, a management tool," said Insley.

THE HEART OF HONDA TQM

What Kawamoto got when he dedicated the company's entire energies to TQM was a simple model for organizational change and management review. Honda's brand of TQM takes a leader's vision and from it sets a business plan that cascades all the way down through the company into every area of operations. When Kawamoto announced that the changes he envisioned would take the company from consensus decision-making to systematic TQM management, he knew this basic process change would forever improve bottom-line results. And the strategy worked. Honda took the number three sales position in Japan; company stock rose 157 percent.

TQM leads from data. These seven points form the backbone of all Honda improvement initiatives:

1. What's the plan compared to the actual?

2. What's the gap?

3. The gap analysis

4. Gap countermeasure

5. The means—money, resources, or people?

6. Who is responsible?

7. When—what is the schedule for completion of each task?

With each iteration of Honda's TQM Spiral, improvements appear. Each spiral represents another Plan, Do, Check, Act circle; at the top of the spiral, associates are looking at four to five priority items. The process itself clarifies thinking and implementation goals.

ONE GLOBAL PHILOSOPHY—
THE COMPANY PRINCIPLE

Co-author Dave Nelson remembers the shock he experienced years ago when, coming from TRW's systems-focused operations, he landed at Marysville. "We didn't have a Bill of Material system, and we didn't even have a cost system. Everything was manual! How could Honda possibly succeed with no systems? What was the glue that kept all that stuck together? Any American company would have said, 'If you don't have a Bill of Material you can't even make cars!' The success came from the philosophies that we believe in. They caused the incredible effort, and the incredible ability to level up."

Figure 3.4   The Basic Plan Do Check Act Spiral

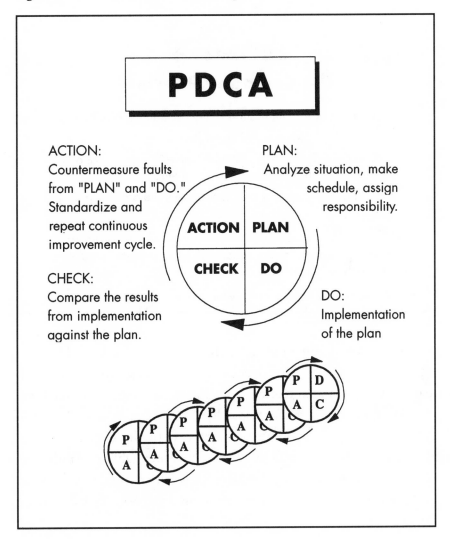

How did Honda get this far without very sophisticated and powerful systems? The answer lies in the superb technical capabilities and expertise of the people, all framed in 23 words that have guided company growth for over 40 years—the Company Principle—(see Figure 3.5).

Figure 3.5   The Company Principle

HONDA
The Company Principle

Maintaining an international viewpoint [think broadly]
We are dedicated [the team]
To supplying products of the highest efficiency yet at a
reasonable price [the method]
For worldwide customer satisfaction [why we are doing this]

Philosophy: Maintaining an international viewpoint translated to creating international regions, each of which designs, produces, and markets to its own customers.

Copyright Honda of America Mfg. Reprinted with the permission of Honda of America Mfg.

As an international business, Honda wants to take full advantage of the opportunities that lie in purchasing where its plants manufacture, and manufacturing in the heart of its customer base. It makes good business sense, socially and politically, as well as providing a currency hedge, to co-locate with the customer base. Honda's localization strategy reduces the inevitable possibility of line shutdowns caused by catastrophes such as Toyota's disastrous brake supplier fire or Nissan's problems with Mexico's currency fluctuations.

TRIAL BY FIRE

On Saturday, February 1, 1997, flames ripped through Toyota brake supplier Aisin Seiki's Kariya plant. By Wednesday, February 5, just four days later, all of Toyota's plants and many of its suppliers were shut down. Japan's Economic Planning Agency calculated that the fire cut the nation's industrial output by 0.1 percent for each day that Toyota was down.[2]

Toyota builds approximately 16,200 vehicles per day in Japan. Because Toyota Japan single-sourced this critical component to Aisin Seiki, and the company had no back-up plan to continue just-in-time deliveries should disaster (earthquake, fire, trucking strike) happen, the results were disastrous. Although Toyota's U.S. and European assembly plants were not expected to be shut down, catching up would take weeks, even months, and the premium would be high. Peter Boardman of UBS Securities Ltd. in Tokyo estimated the cost of shutdown reached $40 million per day.[3]

FALLOUT

Aisin Seiki sells 80 percent of its products to Toyota, and none of its other 12 Japanese plants produce these brake parts. Mitsubishi Motors reportedly halted production of some 4,500 cars, and Suzuki ran short. One estimate of lost output for Toyota exports to the United States totaled 10,000 Camrys, RAV4s, 4Runners, and Lexus out of 40,000 planned for the month of February—25 percent of the U.S. export target.

Clearly the disaster and the recovery cost Toyota, Aisin Seiki, the supplier, and other customers, as well as consumers, millions, as well as lost market share. By the time Toyota came back on-line, the company had lost production of 72,000 vehicles. And Toyota promised suppliers that jumped to the rescue a bonus totaling over $100 million.[4]

HONDA'S TRIAL BY FIRE, THE WEK STORY

WEK Plastics had been successfully supplying Honda for over 15 years when on October 31, 1994, disaster struck. John Cope, HAM manager for manufacturing purchasing, was awakened at 7:00 A.M. that Sunday with the news that WEK's Painesville, Ohio, plant—one of Honda's original eight suppliers—had burned to the ground. WEK was the major supplier of air ducts and other molded plastic parts for the Accord and Civic, along with parts for motorcycles and ATVs. These parts could not be added after vehicle assembly. This was a line-down situation.

Cope moved fast to evaluate the crisis and prepare a situation analysis. All production at WEK was lost, buried under $10 million of rubble, along with tooling and three trailers loaded with parts. Marysville had a one-and-one-half-day supply of Accord parts, and a two-and-one-half-day supply for Civic.

Go to the Spot

Within two hours, a Honda team assembled at WEK to get a fix on inventory in process and in transit, to pull tooling records and process charts, and to strategize. Cope called Japan to line up relief sourcing.

Susan Insley remembers that the first decision was not to shut down, but to "juggle production schedules, sequences, shifts." Two Honda Japan suppliers, Nihon Plas and Kumi Kasei, started daily airlifts of some parts into Ohio, working 24 hours to fill the pipeline.

Federal fire investigators had roped off the fire scene, but they were persuaded to allow Honda associates to move mountains of debris so that engineers could examine the molds. Some had melted, but two-thirds were salvageable. Normal time to rebuild a mold is 5 to 7 days, but the first, and most critical, mold was turned around, checked out, and ready for production in 15 hours.

The entire disaster became a team recovery effort as Honda, WEK, other suppliers, and former suppliers pitched in to keep the Honda lines running. WEK President Walt Kalberer shifted operations to his second Ohio plant and off-loaded a toy manufacturer's work.

By Wednesday, the first mold was back in production, and one week after the fire, with operations back to normal, Honda lost production time had totaled less than one day.

Cope credits teamwork and Honda's go-to-the-spot philosophy, along with its international sourcing flexibility, with keeping losses manageable. "Having teams on-site really cut down on any possibility of miscommunication. Questions about a tool or procedure were answered immediately. Teams on location had authority to make decisions."

For Honda, the final chapter to this crisis includes purchasing follow-up on tool trials, and analysis on the company's recovery process itself. HAM performed more in-depth risk management and developed better methods to evaluate supplier disaster recovery plans. The presence of sprinklers, heat detectors, and fire doors, especially in the plastics industry, has become a prerequisite for meeting Honda's expectations. Further, Honda insurance experts studied the response to various regional risks such as ice storms and tornadoes, not uncommon for Tennessee and Kentucky producers.

JIT (just-in-time) and other lean production management techniques work. But like the girl with the curl in the middle of her forehead, when she was good, she was very, very good, but when she was bad, she was horrid. JIT is designed, like most production systems, to work well under "normal" conditions. When strikes, natural disasters, and other crises happen, companies learn the value of their international, global partnerships. John Cope remembers, "It was a real test for Honda of America, and it was one that really tested the maturity of our organization, our ability to react."

Toyota, GM, and other producers will do well to study and compare the Aisin Seiki and the WEK fire stories.

Lesson Number One:
Maintaining an International Viewpoint
Single-Source but Dual Capability

Single-source, dual capability among suppliers is a minimum requirement for Honda JIT performance. JIT producers must develop a robust Sourcing Strategy that includes costs beyond parts costs, i.e., factory costs, expedite costs, and human costs. When federal fire officials released the WEK molds to Honda associates, they did it knowing that holding up the rebuilding of those molds would have put 70,000 Ohioans out of work. Purchasing professionals must evaluate the costs of supporting a risky supplier, or surviving a tornado or earthquake or fire. Your risk-analysis strategy must begin at the time of supplier evaluation, along with strategic backup planning.

Risk-assessment strategy extends beyond the maxim "don't put all your eggs in one basket." The concept of single sourcing is frequently misunderstood to mean "cut the order and hope," but a combination of self-reliant suppliers and a resilient international supply network in which flexibility allows key players to move as necessary to different parts production is the appropriate JIT sourcing principle.

LESSON NUMBER TWO:
PHILOSOPHY—WE ARE DEDICATED

Dedication shows commitment, pride, and ownership, the way Mark Vernon, purchasing associate working the WEK fire, traveled with the molds the minute they were lifted out of the ruins at WEK. Mark had expected to take his son trick-or-treating, but he knew that if he could transfer the molds to Durivage Pattern and Manufacturing, Inc. in Williston, Ohio, there was a good chance that they would be back on-line within a day or two. Teams on-site made themselves available to answer pattern-maker questions, and, in fact, the first mold was completed in 15 hours.

Dedicated associates, at the spot, took authority and responsibility for running the recovery. Purchasing VPs stayed in Marysville; one, in fact, who was on vacation in Alaska, heard the full story by phone, and, knowing his team was fully in control, stayed there!

LESSON NUMBER THREE:
PHILOSOPHY—TO SUPPLY PRODUCTS
OF THE HIGHEST EFFICIENCY YET
AT A REASONABLE PRICE

It is unusual for a company principle to include a method that tells associates what kind of products to make, and at what price. Chrysler, for example, declares that it will make cars at the lowest possible cost. Honda says, "We are not going to make a cheap product, but we will make a product that the customer thinks has value."

Consider the resale values on comparable vehicles—the Civic, the Neon, and the Escort—Honda products clearly retain higher resale and lower maintenance costs longer over the life of ownership.

What does "the highest efficiency" mean to automakers? Honda believes that it, of course, implies highest quality—an admission ticket to the game—but it means so much more: new technologies, new materials, and higher performance.

Former HAM president Shoichiro Irimajiri demonstrated the reality of product efficiency by disassembling three competitors' engines—the Nova, the Mercedes 190, and the Ford Escort. After cleaning up the parts, he grouped the engine parts in like groups, all valves here, all pistons there, all crankshafts, etc. Part by part, group by group, he explained to associates what was different about each one. In the crankshaft pile, for example, Honda (years before any other producer of mass production engines adopted this technology) started making engines with a forged crankshaft cut from a single piece of steel. Other producers' cast-iron crankshafts proved longer and heavier. Forged steel is compact, stronger, a piece of art that produces less friction as it turns and shows higher output with better fuel economy and gas mileage.

Although castings may be half the cost of forgings, and easier to produce, in the ten years since Honda pioneered this engine breakthrough and localized production in the United States, several producers, including Toyota, have adopted it.

By the 1990 model year, Honda made all engines from aluminum—the block, head, water jacket. Cast iron, the accepted material for other producers, is cheaper, but its weight raises fuel consumption and costs consumers more for gas. Aluminum production is a more challenging technology. Transmission cases are aluminum also—higher output, less weight, and lower fuel consumption.

Lesson Number Four: Philosophy—For Worldwide Customer Satisfaction

HAM Marysville exports 20 percent of its annual production, including right-hand-drive vehicles. To the associates and suppliers, says Insley, "Think about what you do every day. Just remember that there is a little piece of you and Bellefontaine [Ohio] in the quality of that product that you are sending overseas. So when I see a car on the street in Tokyo, and I know it was produced in Ohio, I think of all those fine companies that make up the supply base in Ohio—part of the whole chain of customer satisfaction. Remember, some of those customers are not just in America, they are in all parts of the world."

Imagine the role of purchasing at each of the component suppliers. Purchasing must sit in a swivel chair, looking upstream toward the suppliers and downstream to very demanding customers. Purchasing must maintain a two-way relationship between the supplier and Honda, and be the window to the world. Purchasing associates must understand and translate schedules three times per week, and they must understand and explain what the world is for the supplier. Purchasing occupies a pivotal role in worldwide customer satisfaction.

The Americas Strategy

As a leading global organization, Honda's Global Five-Part Strategy includes strengthening each regional area—Asia, Japan, Europe, and the Americas—to build self-reliance. Each region assumes

Figure 3.6   The Americas Strategy

The Americas Strategy: Evolution of a Global Company

■   Import products from the mother country.

■   Copy production in the local market.

■   Growth of R&D and production engineering in local market.

■   Establish a global network among strong regional operations.

Copyright Honda of America Mfg. Reprinted with the permission of Honda of America Mfg.

---

responsibility for sales and manufacturing operations within its own region. Further, each region may support other regions, as Japanese and Ohio operations demonstrated in the WEK fire recovery, in a global network of complementary supply. First set forth in 1994, this growth strategy, the Americas' Strategy, has resulted in dramatic increases in auto, engine, and drivetrain production in North America and South America, as well as significant new responsibilities for Honda suppliers.

Self-reliance is essential to the successful execution of these plans. Dave King, Senior Manager in the Americas Planning Group and a purchasing veteran, believes that BP and benchmarking are two key elements. King feels that first the organization will identify key characteristics that must be measured and improved. Understanding the capabilities and opportunity areas in each region (stampings, for example, or high-quality plastic molding) will allow efficient allocation of resources and expertise. The challenge of rapid growth means that careful application of experienced resources will continue to be important.

> *"The setting of a goal is the*
> *expression of a commitment."*
>
> Soichiro Honda

How did a small company, an upstart innovator outside the bounds of industry alliances, in less than 50 years revolutionize purchasing and the way cars are designed and built? How did this David take on the Goliaths of motorcycle production and economy car production, and later high-end luxury vehicles? The answer lies in the way great leaders motivate—they set a vision, set a goal, and the results follow. If you build it, they will come. Honda's company principle and its supporting supplier development philosophy, and especially its very powerful and simple BP activities, point the way.

4

The Competitive Challenge—the Race to Give the Customer What He Wants

"It will be interesting to see if the industry can catch up to the leaders and accept the challenge of exceeding owner expectations, since just meeting expectations is obviously no longer enough if a nameplate intends to stay truly competitive in the marketplace and improve overall performance satisfaction levels."

J.D. Power & Associates,
"1990 Vehicle Performance Study"

INTRODUCTION

The auto industry is struggling with a galaxy of challenges. First are "foreign competition" and, for some producers, rising labor costs. Customer loyalty, quality, and price demands are the visible signals of a successful strategy. How each major producer and supplier meets these demands over the next three to five years will determine who wins the race and who is still standing on the track when the flag goes down.

Complex solutions to lean manufacturing betray the simple power that lies in the hearts and minds of the true experts—the empowered employees who, like Rocio in Chapter 1, live day to day with the pressures of the industry. Recognize that suppliers, especially those at the second, third, and even fourth tiers, need help. A one-size-fits-all approach won't work with all partners. Honda BP is a solution that obtains impressive results fast as it builds supplier self-reliance.

STANLEY, DeSOTO, PACKARD, STUDEBAKER, RAMBLER ...

The history of the auto industry is littered with companies that grew for a time and then died. 1996, the year that marked the one hundredth anniversary of the U.S. auto industry, signaled a turning point for competitors. One hundred years after Charles and Frank Duryea started their first 13-car production run, the industry is a battleground of fierce competition on a field of technology, customer, market, and production changes.

Dedication to excellence in only one of these areas will not guarantee financial gains, or even survival. Chrysler learned from its extremes of parts and model proliferation. Ford's organizational boundaries that became barriers to global growth have been torn down and rebuilt. Mazda's pioneering use of robotics was insufficient to carry the company forward. Mercedes Benz, once the gold-plated symbol of luxury performance, has also rethought its organization and parts production methods. Nissan's understated production strengths are challenged by other equally skilled competitors. For Subaru and Mitsubishi, a niche strategy may be enough in the United States to maintain a toehold, but not enough to win the race. Volkswagen's rock-solid "car of the people" approach is faltering, with no clear answer in sight. Even Toyota's universally admired and copied production system is being redesigned. Not one of the survivors of the current car wars is guaranteed a place in the next millenium's lineup.

The Game of Corporate Chicken

When David Halberstam predicted in *The Reckoning* that the automotive world would experience tremendous upheavals in the 90s, he foresaw a dangerous supply/demand imbalance—five cars for every four buyers—a buyer's market. That imbalance is playing itself out in a race among giants. None of the competitors wants to back off because backing off would mean cutting supply and shutting down plants. The competitors have created strategies for capturing finite demand that include competitive pricing, product innovation, aggressive marketing, nurturing of customer loyalty, and old-fashioned price cutting.

But what is the perfect combination of technology, features, price, quality, service, and availability that attracts and retains customers for life? Unfortunately, too often the answer is a single mechanical approach to better quality or lowered costs. Remember industry's MRP (Material Requirements Planning) crusades in the late 70s? The overwhelming winners here were the software vendors. Or how about our brief fascination with finite scheduling modules? Here, the complexity bred further complexity. A single-minded approach to manufacturing excellence drove many naive adopters to endless struggles with complexity, never-ending computer training classes, and expensive consulting assists that frequently became permanent dependencies. There is no balance here.

The 80s saw many companies stage periodic forays into complex, theoretical approaches to business, an OR (operations research) MacNamaraian construct crammed with grand plans and grand speeches that produced grand disappointments. Again, the consultants took home the winnings.

Unfortunately for suppliers, one of the easiest levers big customers reach for first is cost. Where costs for purchased parts typically represent 80 percent of total vehicle cost, the opportunity for "The Big Squeeze"—hammering costs out of the supply base—becomes more and more attractive. Small- and medium-sized suppliers, the backbone of North American industrial growth, responsible for over 95 percent of new jobs, are easy targets.

Each automotive competitor and its suppliers magnify and intensify the cost focus. But their approaches vary. Some producers take the "Lopez approach." Suppliers are hit with nonnegotiable demands for big cost reductions on signed contracts. More than five years after GM purchasing head Ignacio Lopez's 1992 arrival and rapid departure from Detroit, the impact of his heavy-handed approach is still felt. Many suppliers, veterans who have experienced the energy-draining challenge of meeting these demands, have successfully scrambled to build a more diversified, and therefore "less leverageable," customer base.

Other big customers take a more even-handed approach, still

demanding cost cuts, but presenting their requirements in a more tempered, negotiable business context. Although cost cuts remain the objective, the customer places more responsibility for maneuvering around the numbers into the hands of the supplier.

Still others, Honda included, take a more proactive and simpler approach to manufacturing excellence, cost reduction, and improved performance. Cost cuts are not a simple function of headcount reductions, or better raw material prices, or even state-of-the art capital equipment. Better processes produce better products. Better processes cut waste and reduce unit costs.

Because Honda understands that not all suppliers have the resources to make big changes in their processes, and inevitably cut costs, they make available to suppliers a range of in-house expertise—from safety consultants to small-business attorneys and quality circle competitions and training. Their goal is twofold:

To raise the bar, by bringing quality and delivery performance up to near-perfect levels among all suppliers, and

Self-reliance, to ensure that the methods for complete self-reliance become part of the supplier's culture, to develop supplier self-reliance.

BP, Honda's premier supplier development program, inevitably removes waste, the end result of which is lowered costs. The overall stated objective of the program is not, first of all, cost reduction. BP is designed to improve the process. Although the spirit of continuous improvement means that the process is never perfect, from a better process profits follow.

FACING UP TO INDUSTRY-WIDE CHALLENGES

At all tiers, the automotive industry, or more correctly the people-moving machine, is being swept along by technology changes, marketplace changes, and heightened customer expectations. And two major weaknesses have always existed:

1. *The failure to appreciate the importance of new technology.* New technologies have a way of finding their place. GPS (global positioning systems), a Cold War aerospace innovation, for example, may not appear on all customer wish lists, but most drivers welcome a scaled down system as a cost-effective navigational aid. Seat belts, air bags, remanufacturing of recyclable cars—each of these technology advances took years to reach marketable levels.

2. *The failure to anticipate changes in the marketplace, and to adjust to changing customer expectations quickly.* Just as Detroit in the 60s mistakenly remained wedded to gas guzzlers, so today are automakers challenged to anticipate the next wave of human needs embodied by the auto. Car distribution networks of competing franchises connected by cooperative marketing, or sales "pushers," will be restructured as customers continue to demand more service and as they begin to participate in their car's design.

Technology will continue to change the way the workplace looks, how it works, how people communicate within it. Technology is power, but technology can displace and shake up workforce roles; technology can blur decades of carefully constructed roles. In the design area, for example, automotive stylist jobs are touching on the domain of process engineers and designers. Indeed, as 3-D design capabilities improve exponentially, the design area will redefine when and how much virtual design work will replace thousands of hours of skilled human judgment and creativity. Just as Boeing's 777 "paperless aircraft" design pioneered and perfected the design cycle, changes in the way clay models and subsequent design iterations are done in automotive will improve the process.

IT'S A TEAM GLOBAL EFFORT

Technology and other big changes for automotive do not flourish in
a vacuum. Customers, suppliers, and competitors are learning it's a
team sport, and the best team wins. So the question for the entire
industry—competitors and suppliers alike—is how should automotive manufacturers and their suppliers work together to meet the
demands of this changing environment?

First, the industry must develop leading-edge technology that
generates products faster, more efficiently, and with greater value for
the customer. Technology holds the key to six-month or sooner
new model introductions. Technology is providing the answers to
Toyota's Three-Day Car Challenge, and technology will make
customer-designed vehicles a reality. Technology will change the
dealer franchise marketing and distribution system into a customer-
driven entity.

Technology, however, has varying impacts at different tiers in the
industry. At the first tier, companies like Honda, Motorola, Ford,
and Hewlett Packard have been working for years to develop lean
manufacturing methods, to dedicate training hours to their workforce, and to constantly seek the advantageous technology edge.
In the ten years since Motorola won the first Baldrige Award,
industry leaders have tackled challenges that extend beyond the
question of Six Sigma quality; they have knitted a durable fabric
of manufacturing technologies, clean, agile factories, with vision
and an empowered workforce. And the results speak well of their
efforts.

But what about the second, third, and fourth tiers in the automotive industry?

CHALLENGE NUMBER ONE

Suppliers need help. Although they are the experts in their product and process area, most small- and medium-sized companies cannot support wide-ranging technology initiatives or big workforce training programs on their own. Further, although they are inevitably driven by their very demanding customers to adopt new methods, many smaller companies are hard-pressed to strategically decide which particular new technique or method is the one to which they should dedicate their limited resources. Should they concentrate on work flow redesign, or kanban, or workforce literacy, or fast setup changes? And what will be the cost, should a small- or medium-sized company make a commitment to the wrong technology package?

For help, suppliers instead look to supplier associations, to the academic community, to government, to industry groups, occasionally to other suppliers, and finally, to their customers.

But which source of help is most effective? Big customers use big training programs, tailored for their specific workforce and marketplace. Does a big company's training program fit its smaller colleagues? We think not. The workforce, the environment, and the focus at Massachusetts plastics-producer Nypro, for example, an excellent second-tier supplier to Hewlett Packard, differs very much from the workforce of its world-class customer.

Although Hewlett Packard and Nypro share a customer focus and dedication to zero defect quality, HP is an assembler, and Nypro is an expert at plastics technology, occupying a strategic position at the very beginning of the production flow. Nypro's pioneering use of real-time, fully automated control systems in production is a lesson in the difference between monitoring and manual feedback mechanisms, and automation that produces Nypro's recognized near-perfect quality. Hewlett Packard's challenges, such as its parts count and new product offerings, are more complex than Nypro's. Just as Hewlett Packard has become one of the U.S. premier electronics companies, so has Nypro taken a quality leadership role within its own industry.

Each competitor must perfect elements particular to its own strategic focus. In the case of HP, that current focus is fast, multiple new-product innovation, at consistently high quality, within a market to which the company can rightfully claim ownership. Hewlett Packard's supplier/partner Nypro's strategy, however, is building excellent partnerships with a limited number of Fortune 500 partners. That strategy embodies Nypro's "MacDonald's approach" to manufacturing. The company locates new plants, each of which maintains a high degree of self-reliance, including its own board of directors and president, side-by-side with each major customer, such as Abbott Labs in Chicago and Hewlett Packard's Vancouver Ink Jet plant.

One Size Does Not Fit All

So, a one-size-fits-all approach to supplier excellence won't fit. And other approaches, many of which cost hundreds of thousands of dollars per implementation, continue to miss the mark. Can government small-business competitiveness initiatives give small- and medium-sized suppliers what they need to reach zero defect performance levels?

In the early 90s, the U. S. government freed up millions in DARPA/ARPA monies to help small- and medium-sized businesses become more competitive by improving their manufacturing operations. A burst of nonprofit, consulting/training offerings, networks, and national laboratories grew from that initiative, with mixed success. The New England Suppliers Institute (NESI), for example, boasts documented supplier success stories from a range of industries, including stamping, printed circuit board, and plastics. These few shining success stories, however, are not enough.

The best and most-lasting programs are those that teach suppliers how to improve on their own. Honda suppliers TRW, Parker Hannifin, and Donnelly Corporation, for example, epitomize companies that have experienced BP and have absorbed its principles into their own culture.

CHALLENGE NUMBER TWO

In the age of globalization, companies must adopt a world view that extends beyond domestic markets. Local suppliers command local expertise, and JIT production and local markets demand globally distributed manufacturing excellence.

CHALLENGE NUMBER THREE

Competitors must frame all their actions in terms of what the customer expects from the industry, and then exceed these expectations. Zero defect quality is merely the ticket that admits competitors to the games.

Technology Provides Some Answers

Technology drives the motor-vehicle industry. Technology has provided tools to make cars and their components safer, more durable, and more efficient. Technology has improved the manufacturing process, from inflexible batch-driven production flows to single-unit, mixed model production that would confound Henry Ford. Technology has taken over pieces of the production process, like welding and painting, areas in which human hands find it impossible to compete with robotic arms.

Technology has changed the workforce, as it has made the auto plant a safer and more interesting place to work.

Further, technology has also created more powerful communications tools that, properly enabled, allow us to share information quickly, globally, and in great detail. In the design area, for example, iterative development of elegant designs, leading to clay models, followed by measurement and conversion to manufacturable designs, each from a separate functional "expert," will give way to an integrated, multifunctional design-to-production approach similar to Boeing's pioneering 777 "paperless aircraft."

Yet each automotive assembler and supplier continues to look for new technology to bring greater value to customers. The goal is to cut leadtime, costs, and defects. Honda knows that because technology is key to the company's 50-year rise, sharing it with business partners makes good business sense. The company's history, starting with its leadership in the motorcycle market, exemplifies its technology-driven energy.

Staying on Top of Technology

Honda continues to look to new technology to bring greater value to customers, to cut leadtime, slash costs, reduce defects, and increase efficiency. And now, the future success of manufacturers and suppliers depends on how well the entire extended enterprise collaborates on technology challenges. Technological partnerships are absolutely essential.

Suppliers Drive VTEC
Engine Technology Breakthroughs

A good example is one of Honda's newest engines, the three liter-V6 engine for the new Acura CL sport-luxury coupe, the first North American designed and produced vehicle among Honda's new product offerings. This engine is the lightest, most compact, and most powerful engine in its class. It is also the first single-overhead cam V6 to employ Honda's high-technology variable-valve VTEC technology.

This breakthrough in engine technology tore down another barrier—it went from the drawing board to mass production in about 24 months, one full year less than the usual development time for a new Honda engine, and six months ahead of the typical industry average. Suppliers' early involvement was one of the main drivers for this success.

For example, Honda supplier Zenith Sintered Products in Germantown, Wisconsin, developed a new powdered metal bearing cap for this project. Honda R & D—both in Ohio and in Japan—worked closely with Zenith to develop the new bearing cap, a design that improved NVH (noise, vibration, and handling) characteristics, reduced development cost compared to traditional cast-iron bearing caps, and saved Honda the cost of a new $11 million machining line.

Eaton Corporation in Marshall, Michigan, developed a more efficient, cost-effective design in Honda's VTEC variable-valve system—the lost motion mechanism. Engineers at Eaton improved on this part of Honda's proprietary technology by developing a three-piece design to replace Honda's five-piece design, and by using cold-forming technology prevalent in the United States. The result was reduced machining operations.

A third supplier example, Burgess-Norton in Geneva, Illinois, developed a full-floating piston pin that reduced noise, simplified engine assembly, and cut cost.

Finally, CWC Castings of Battle Creek, Michigan, worked with Honda to develop a flame-hardening process for the ductile iron camshafts used in the new V6 engine. Previous Honda V6 designs used a chilled block casting for the camshaft. The new process saved manufacturing time and cut costs.

New ideas. New technologies. Partnerships. No one entity can generate this kind of energy alone.

Survival Means the Best Team Wins

Over 50 years ago, in March 1947, Soichiro Honda, at age 40, having worked with engines most of his life, was trying to develop a real motorcycle, one that would take the place of the bicycles he had retrofitted with small war surplus engines. The first prototype, completed in August 1949, was greeted by Mr. Honda and his 20 employees with great celebration. "It's like a dream!" the fitting name for his first design, and his bigger dream—to become a global automotive producer.

But there were many technical and human barriers to be scaled first. By 1948, when Honda Technical Research Institute became Honda Motor, the company produced two engine types—the 50cc and the 98cc. Two years later the company acquired a bigger factory in which it produced a succession of more powerful motorcycles. Honda wanted to enter the auto industry next, but Japanese Ministry of trade (MITI) policies that limited entry of new producers stood as another barrier to innovation.

Mr. Honda turned to his motorcycle suppliers, asking them to supply auto components, technically not that big a departure from their current operations, but an era away from the dream's beginnings. The suppliers stood by him and pitched in to help. Blocked by other traditional automotive suppliers from entering automotive production, an industry which Mr. Honda believed was ripe for innovation and new challenges, Honda found its true partners in its network of motorcycle components suppliers. And he never forgot that mutual dependency and shared spirit between customer and supplier. Individually, neither the suppliers nor Honda would have succeeded in building a global giant. Together, they formed a team that matured and competed successfully, globally, in a succession of tough races.

Success in the automotive challenge comes to those suppliers and producers who work with their partners to develop and apply new technology, and create increased value for the customer. Two newer concepts continue to challenge management—technology adoption and partnering. Acceptance of new technology as a concept makes business sense, but on a personal level, many executives are challenged by the newness of the idea.

Most of us are periodically challenged to learn new word-processing software. It's a struggle. It makes us yearn for the 200-pound Underwood (another company on the "dear departed" list). The comfort of a manual typewriter's metallic clatter, the pure physical effort required to produce a single page, is hard to replace with a laptop's extreme touch sensitivity and its multifunction electronic menus.

But even though technology does not always come easy to most of us over the age of three, we know that we have a personal responsibility to the people we work with to learn new ways to do our jobs better. Technology becomes a personal issue, as well as a business one. Until we bridge the gap between our acceptance of technology as a business tool, and our acceptance—our embrace of technology as individuals—we will never reach the full potential that technology offers.

Industry leaders accept and promote new ideas, new perspectives, and new technologies. Understanding and accepting new ideas is crucial as the auto industry moves into new markets, new alliances, and new competitive challenges. But sharing or collaborating as an enterprise team is very hard, as GM, Volkswagen, GE, and other giants continue to discover.

Survival means that the best team wins, and the winner takes all. In a global economy whose geographic and governmental barriers have shrunk to stepping stones, businesses inevitably rub shoulders with competitors, future competitors, one-time partners, and former collaborators. There is nowhere to run.

To survive in the global economy, your organization must have a basic and enduring philosophy that emphasizes the importance of having an international field of vision. At Honda, that has been the viewpoint for fifty years. The Honda company principle written in 1948 guides strategic growth as the company takes marketing, production, design, and distribution to new world markets.

The company principle led Honda to begin manufacturing in the United States in 1979—a time of the strong dollar and the weak yen—in an era in which great skepticism about the quality of

Figure 4.1   Global Stepping Stones

American motor vehicles ruled. The American worker was under fire, and the idea of asking a small group of workers from the American Midwest to build Honda's first product offerings seemed impossible.

Honda proceeded with its decision—based on the company principle—to invest in U.S. manufacturing. Wall Street did not make this decision, neither were there pounds of justification embedded in lengthy marketing and economic analysis studies. The decision to start production in Marysville, Ohio, the crossroads of the American Midwest, was not a Wall Street decision. It was a Main Street decision, supported by data and site analysis, straight from the gut. Honda motorcycles and Civics were being well-received by American customers. There was already an established sales network in America. So it made sense that American workers should enjoy the opportunity to produce vehicles where they were needed.

Supplier Quality Is All-Important

The typical family four-door sedan contains an average of 6,000 components and assemblies. Honda's supply base in North America, feeding the Marysville/East Liberty Auto Plant, totals more than 400 suppliers for all facilities and products, almost all of whom are located within 3 hours of the plants. With production rates of over 400 vehicles per shift per line, and one vehicle coming off every line every minute, the costs of line-down situations anywhere on the assembly line or further upstream in the supply chain is extremely high per minute per line. If a supplier delivers the wrong part number, bad quality or bad paperwork, or if the transportation system breaks down, for even a period of ten minutes, the costs mount up.

Clearly, production of Accords in Ohio is completely dependent on hundreds of upstream connections and material transfers. And yet, amazingly, parts quality levels continue to rise—quality as measured and reported by Honda includes on-time delivery—to undreamed of levels from all types of suppliers.

Supplier quality initiatives have always had great importance at Honda. Indeed, in 1987, during the early years of the Marysville plant when there were less than 100 OEM (original equipment manufacturing) suppliers, Jackie Hammonds, one of the pioneers of this initiative, worked with 15 of the suppliers to produce quality circle presentations in which teams gained company-wide recognition for their quality improvement ideas that were implemented successfully and at a reasonable cost.

As the number of suppliers and quality circles grew, so did the number of companies trained in quality processes by Honda. In 1995, there were 242 companies targeted for quality circle training. By fiscal 1995, when the quality circle training target was 1,000, a total of 1,151 associates had been trained in a mix of management seminars (4 hours), quality circle orientation (16 hours), quality circle tools (8 hours), and the Five Ps (8 hours).

Especially important to all problem-solving activities, inside Honda, and at its suppliers, are "The Five Principles for Problem Solving," Honda's version of problem-solving techniques that enable associates to capture the experiences gained during problem-solving on a single 11" × 17" worksheet. The worksheet helps associates focus on root cause and assigns permanent countermeasures.

Brad Robinson, administrative coordinator in Associate Services at Honda of Canada Manufacturing, Inc., the new Alliston, Ontario plant, traces the role quality initiatives have played in Honda's global growth. "NH [New Honda] Circles develop self-reliance...it is important for associates to continue making improvements... because the associates know best the reality of their work areas. They have the most knowledge of their work areas, and they are in the best position to recommend and implement changes." The fact that Honda manufactures and sells products in many parts of the world requires that associates have the flexibility to meet the needs of different types of markets, and each region of the world needs self-reliance to design and engineer products to meet these needs. As associates expand their skills and knowledge and deepen their understanding of the company's operations, each Honda operation develops a distinct character.

GROWTH, ZERO DEFECTS, ZERO MISDELIVERIES

Honda's BP Program, combined with the company's early years' hours of education, training, and participation in Quality Circles, all yielding solid bottom-line results, rewarded suppliers willing to tackle the journey from acceptable quality levels to Honda's "zero misdeliveries, zero defects" standards. More and more local suppliers grew and perfected their performance. By 1997, more than 90 percent of all purchased parts were supplied by North American suppliers.

Quality Pays Off

The quality focus has immediate impact on any supplier or Honda associate it touches. Each spring, all of Honda of America's suppliers gather for the annual supplier conference for a plant tour, speeches summarizing the new challenges, their quality "report cards," and plain old-fashioned networking. The 1996 event offered exponential opportunities to suppliers who had made a commitment to supply Honda. As auto and motorcycle production has increased exponentially, so has supplier opportunity.

Along with this growth opportunity come increased demands on parts quality. The Anna Engine Plant alone, for example, has raised its production target from 500,000 units per year to 750,000 by 1998, then 900,000/year. Five categories of performance recognition signal supplier excellence.

Fifteen suppliers in 1997 won quality performance awards, in a variety of commodity groups; twenty-four suppliers achieved zero

Figure 4.2   Supplier Awards

The Quality Performance Award

To qualify for this award, suppliers must be at the top of their commmodity type measured by quality rejects ppm (parts per million). Other quality criteria include severity of quality rejects measured by indexing and superior delivery performance.

Delivery Performance Award

This award is presented to those suppliers who have achieved 0 parts per million misdeliveries combined with superior quality performance.

Productivity Improvement Award

This award is presented to the suppliers who have improved productivity, including items such as improving yield rates or reducing cycle times, which have resulted in cost improvement.

Production Support Award

This award is presented to those raw material suppliers who have overall high performance in quality, delivery, and cost.

Double Award Winners

Suppliers may win quality and delivery awards, or delivery and product improvement awards.

misdeliveries; eleven suppliers were double-award winners, twenty-four won productivity improvement recognition, and one raw material supplier was recognized for overall high performance in quality, delivery, and cost. These suppliers, and dozens of other years' winners, have proven that zero defect quality is achievable.

Clearly, production of complex machines from thousands of parts supplied by hundreds of different companies requires a team effort, a unified approach driven by a few commonly held standards and operating philosophies. Although not all of Honda's 400-plus suppliers resemble one another physically, neither do they mirror their customers' own culture. All Honda team members share a fierce competitive spirit and an intense dedication to the task at hand. They understand that the best team wins.

BUILDING THE WINNING TEAM

> *"Racing is so challenging that you can never win without teamwork. Teamwork is the common keyword for Indy team members and NH Circle members."*
> Nobuhiko Kawamoto, President, Honda Motor Co., NH Circles World Convention, Columbus, Ohio, 1996

Racing—motorcycles, Formula I cars, and now Indy cars—has always driven Honda and exemplifies the passion that has built this global innovator. The company's leadership has consistently been drawn from the ranks of engineers who love engines and who share a passion to drive well-designed, robust, high-speed vehicles to their limits and beyond.

Hands-on Development

Soichiro Honda received thorough grounding in auto repair during the 1920s and 1930s at a service station in Hamamatsu. The shop's owner, Mr. Sakakibara, also had a passion for racing, and he encouraged young Honda to build a racer at night. Powered by a Curtis-Wright aircraft engine, with 100 horsepower revving at 1400 rpm, the car took Honda into the winner's circle many times.

Honda's next project, a modified Ford engine, ended his racing career, but not his belief in the power of high-performance, high-revving racing machines. On his last lap in the 1936 All-Japan Speed

Figure 4.3   Past CEOs/Presidents Who Have Been Involved in Racing

Past CEOs/Presidents Who Have Been Involved in Racing		
NAME	**TITLE**	**ACTIVITY**
Soichiro Honda	Founder and President of Honda Motor Company	Raced as a young man and continued his interest throughout his life
Tadashi Kume	Former President of Honda Motor Company	Key member of the FI racing R & D teams
Nobuhiko Kawamoto	President and CEO of Honda Motor Company	Motorcycle Grand Prix and Auto FI racing involvement with Honda R & D
Shoichiro Irimajiri	Former EVP of Honda Motor and Former President of Honda of America Mfg.	Designer, Engineer, and Key Director—Motorcycle Grand Prix and Auto FI racing
Hiroyuki Yoshino	EVP of Honda Motor Company and Former President of Honda of America Mfg.	Involved with FI racing with Honda R & D
Takeo Fukui	Current President of Honda of America Mfg.	Motorcycle Grand Prix director of racing program during the 70s, when Honda won several world championships

Rally, moving at over 75 mph, Honda's new design collided with a car coming out of a pit stop. The crash injured both Mr. Honda (the driver) and his younger brother, but Honda set a Japanese average speed record that remained unbroken for almost 20 years.

A succession of Honda presidents have raced vehicles, starting with Soichiro Honda, down through Shoichiro Irimajiri, and the current president Nobuhiko Kawamoto (see Figure 4.3), who ran Honda's Formula I racing program. Under the stresses of racing, the driver, his vehicle, and his support team experience their greatest performance peaks. Each race, every lesson, and every failure are treasured.

The Racing Spirit

Honda-powered Indy cars, specially engineered racing vehicles, "land-based rockets" designed to run 200 miles per hour on the Indy circuit, had a very successful season in 1996, and 32-year old Oregonian Parker Johnstone was among the drivers who helped Honda win the Manufacturer's Championship trophy. Johnstone is a model for the professional race car driver of the 90s. His engineering degree makes him particularly valuable as a test and development driver. He appreciates the value of teamwork on and off the track.

Indy cars race on many different tracks, ovals, road courses, and street circuits under many different conditions. The drivers and the pit crew, as well as the engineers, must prepare for a variety of challenges. Their goal is high speed, flexibility, and reliability. Racers typically run their very expensive cars at tough competition up to 230 miles per hour for hours at a time.

International Power Package

Johnstone drives a Reynard chassis built in England, on Firestone tires designed in Japan, made in Ohio by Bridgestone Advanced Manufacturing, on wheels built in Germany, powered by a Honda motor conceived, designed, and built in Japan and maintained in the United States—truly an international effort! But for all the technological wonderment of building and running a successful Indy car race, the common denominator of this internationally designed and built winner is, says Johnstone, "the people behind it, and the competitive spirit they hold in their hearts."

The Honda spirit that is defined by creating the best engineered product possible, and refining it and its engineers and designers through the rigors of racing, is at the center of all true competitors. A typical Indy-car team has about 20 members to support each car—a driver, engineers, team managers, owners, technicians, mechanics, public-relations staff, truck drivers, painters, fabricators—and the whole team must work together effectively to produce the best results possible.

Figure 4.4   Nelson, Johnstone, and Mayo

Not far behind, supporting the race team, come the suppliers—the best research and development, and the technical support personnel that build the chassis, the tires, and the engine. The driver who stands atop the victory podium on Sunday afternoon has achieved victory through the determination of not only his effort and his team's, but the collective efforts of thousands of dedicated professionals.

Unique to Indy car racing is the need for driver, crew, and car to adapt to different kinds of racing circuits such as road courses, street courses, one-mile ovals, and super-speedways. Johnstone is frequently asked to describe the difference between an oval car and a road-race car. "Basically everything," he answers, "the suspension, the aerodynamics, the tires, even the engine and transmission are different between road courses and ovals. The team has to adapt to an entirely different set of challenges in each type of racing circuit that it encounters."

The need for an Indy car team to adapt quickly to changing environments is very similar to Honda's need to respond quickly to regional requirements and customer wishes thoughout the world. Johnstone knows that driving at speeds in excess of 200 miles per hour is the result of the dream achieved through creativity, focus, leadership, hard work, "and the ability of a team—not an individual, but a team—to work through whatever obstacles are presented to them."

Racing is simply a matter of problem solving, and those suppliers and customers who work together best as a team can solve all the problems, but only the best team can win. Honda-powered drivers won the CART Indy-car 1997 driver's championship for the second year in a row. Alex Zenardi of the Chip Gnassi team won. 1996s' winner was veteran Jimmy Vassar.

5

Many Roads Lead to Excellence and the New Partnership

"Racing isn't for every engineer we have out there or every associate, but we need a core group of people within the company with that experience. That's one of the things racing, especially production-based cars, will teach you."
Forrest Granlund, Associate at the Honda East Liberty, Ohio, Auto Plant

INTRODUCTION

Honda's long tradition of auto racing, epitomized by the Racing Spirit, teaches associates hard lessons in being the best, preparing for the competition, teamwork, and learning from mistakes. Every Honda associate and supplier associate is in a very competitive race, and every team member's contribution counts. Honda's tradition of auto and motorcycle race involvement always begins with "an impossible challenge"—the Isle of Man Race, the Formula I circuit, Indy cars, and, internally, the Honda of America Racing Team (HART), whose story follows. Honda Purchasing is also an award-winning organization. How the group finds and develops associates as members of a winning team is key to Honda's continued enterprise-wide success.

Forrest Granlund is a lanky, 35-year-old mechanical engineer at Honda's East Liberty, Ohio, auto plant that produces Civics and Acura CLs. From experience, Granlund understands the passion and determination that it takes to win a sports-car race, the same spirit of concentration, focus, and competitiveness that guides Honda's development of its powerful purchasing organization.

In 1990, Granlund started thinking about the possibility of taking his passion for cars off the street and onto the track. Although he had never raced, he had the feeling that it might be fun. The first step, driving school, was an eye-opener. Next, he assembled a group of Honda associates who persuaded the company to fund the purchase of two used Civic EX Coupes for $6,500. The associates loaded them up with a roll cage, a five-point safety harness, a fire extinguisher, and a window net, and the race was on. Although Granlund fully expected to start off at the amateur level driving showroom stock, he was surprised by the results he and his teammates turned in. Driving their two street-legal Civics to and from the meet, the team learned how to prepare and learn from each experience.

The HART (Honda of America Racing Team), as the small group became known, stripped the hubcaps to eliminate the possibility of leaving broken plastic on the track, taped up the headlights, donned helmets, and laid rubber. In the first year, Granlund won three amateur races sponsored by the Sports Car Club of America— Watkins Glenn, Nelson Ledges, and Mid-Ohio. They were hooked, speed junkies.

Nine events later, Granlund won Ohio Valley Region Rookie Driver of the Year. "It was great, man; I won a clock! Had no idea that I won. I went to the awards banquet just to be with my friends!"

In the fall of 1991, the national championships in Atlanta were a big step for HART. For the first time, having used up all their own vacation time and weekends, the team was allotted time away from work as official representatives of Honda.

"I was very green," Granlund remembers. "My inexperience showed as people pushed me off the track and I ended up going from second to tenth place, fighting back to sixth...a classic case of a good, but inexperienced driver.... People were pushing me off the track, and I remember thinking 'you're not supposed to do that!' I was very nice then, too easy a driver. I followed the rules, but *here I was in a race with 32 crazies and they all wanted to win, and it's a whole different set of rules!*"

WINNING WITH A TEAM

As the team matured, the rules changed even more. Granlund realized the limitations of running a driver-only race. "After the race started, the team was out of it. It became just the driver and the car. All the preparation was done, and the teamwork was done. Now it was only the driver and the car." The crew wanted to tackle a challenge requiring more teamwork, and that challenge was endurance racing, complete with pit stops, crews, strategy, vehicles, and drivers all competing together throughout the race.

In 1991, HART competed in the International Motor Sports Association Firestone Firehawk Endurance Championship, running cars more modified than showroom stock, finishing 13 out of 33 cars. "Testing the waters" grew to a commitment to endurance racing that took the team in a "very noncompetitive car"—a 125-horsepower, 1.6-liter-engine Civic—to the 24-hour Watkins Glen endurance classic, then on to Sebring.

The team had assembled an entire crew, all volunteer Honda associates, with the addition of two recruited professional drivers, one of whom ran a Honda dealership back in Granlund's hometown of State College, Pennsylvania. The rigors of endurance racing opened up a whole new world for the volunteers. "Now we had strategies, we had tire changes, we had brake pad changes, we had fueling. 'Do you come in now or wait?' It brought everybody in and stressed the car to its limits."

This is Honda's Racing Spirit and hands-on learning personified. Granlund's four original objectives—first, learning about Honda products in a harsh environment; second, using racing to develop the associates; third, promoting Honda activities in the United States; and fourth, teaching HAM associates the Racing Spirit—continued to be reinforced as the team moved, in three years, from amateur to professional performance.

THE 3A'S: ACTUAL PLACE, ACTUAL PART, ACTUAL SITUATION

The HART team broke a lot of parts that first year. "We stressed the brakes. The engines ran flawlessly. We saw some of the chassis

*"It's hard to quantify, but racing basi-
cally teaches you 'hands on' about the
car. You see how tough the car is. You
cannot understand the problem unless
you are there. Racing gave me the
opportunity to learn about the parts."*

Forrest Granlund

pieces wear out quick. We broke in rotors. We learned more about
the hub design, the suspension, the brakes, the brake pad material.
It's one thing to come out of college and know the theory about
brake pads. It's another thing to understand what happens when
you heat them extremely high and put extremely high pressures
on, and what happens to the coefficient of friction, what happens to
the rotor surface when it becomes gouged and the rotors get
warped."

Teamwork, Focus, Concentration, and Speed

From Honda's brash entry into the Isle of Man Race, which it won
three years later, to its Formula I, Indy car, and motorcycle racing
successes, to its development of a world-class purchasing organization and a global, world-class supply base, the approach is always
the same. Starting small with big dreams, it's not big money, but
vision, concentration, teamwork, and competitiveness—the Racing
Spirit—that makes winners.

A PHILOSOPHY-DRIVEN TEAM – THE RACING SPIRIT, AND THE HONDA WAY

Every company runs to a formal, stated mission statement, supported with unstated philosophies and procedures, and colored by legends and myths. Honda's basic strategy, starting over 50 years ago with the founder's collaboration with motorcycle suppliers to crack the automotive market and extending down through the company's sixth decade of growth, has been to focus on and hold to the philosophy behind its operations. The philosophy that expresses the company's principles is called The Honda Way.

The Honda Way expresses to employees inside the company, and to suppliers and customers on the outside, how the company does business, what approaches to business relationships are the preferred mode of operation, and how to make day-to-day operating decisions that reflect the company's best objectives.

The Honda Way is the philosophy that guides associates' everyday actions and decision-making, as well as the way associates treat relationships; respect for the individual is the foundation for this philosophy. Associates come to understand that this umbrella-like philosophy helps clarify decisions and good results—the Three Joys. The first joy is the joy of making a high-quality product, the second joy is selling a high-quality and efficient product, and the third joy is buying a good product. Suppliers participate in the execution of these philosophies because they are building Accords and Civics—not parts and not components.

When a supplier builds a steering column, for example, it is building a Honda, not a part. When Honda sells an Accord, although dozens of separate suppliers have contributed to the total vehicle, the customer's perception is limited to the Honda label. When customers are pleased, they speak well of the company, and they usually

---

The Challenging Spirit:
Honda Motor Co., Ltd.
Management Policy

- Proceed always with ambition and youthfulness.

- Respect sound theory, develop fresh ideas, and make the most effective use of time.

- Enjoy your work, and always brighten your working atmosphere.

- Strive constantly for a harmonious flow of work.

- Be ever mindful of the value of research and endeavor.

---

become lifetime owners. If customers have a bad experience, although they do not know the name and location of the problem supplier, they begin to perceive a less than perfect image of the total product.

The new, global order—Honda's global extended enterprise—is based on many alliances, such as teams, customers and suppliers, quality initiatives, and BP projects, that cannot work without trust, communication, sharing of responsibilities and growth, and the synergy that comes from a true understanding of a common goal along with a focused approach to meeting it. How better to manage such diversity than through a philosophy, The Honda Way, that permeates daily operations and extends to the supply base?

The goal is to build a flexible, capable, integrated team, which includes suppliers, that can quickly meet and exceed any challenge, from Indy-car racing to the HART Racing Team to new product introductions like the innovative Acura CL. The new partnership is a global opportunity, spread over Honda's 89 production facilities in 33 countries, supported by thousands of local suppliers.

Clearly, a corporate mission statement translated into dozens of different languages needs other elements to be consistent throughout all its diverse applications. In the North American operations, purchasing performs a major role in the day-to-day execution, the carving and polishing, of the company's role as a leader in its extended enterprise. Honda Purchasing will continue to drive daily operations, even as the company works to build regional self-reliance in its assembly plants and its suppliers.

PATHS TO EXCELLENCE, THE NEW PARTNERSHIP

In 1995, Honda Purchasing was awarded the Medal of Excellence by *Purchasing* magazine "for its true understanding of the value of the supply chain, and for its long-term approach to developing world-class suppliers." Previous winners of the award include Hewlett Packard and Chrysler. The award cited the organization's proven innovation in the profession, starting at the top, as Honda Purchasing demonstrated top management's view of the supply chain. Although Honda works with suppliers in many different ways, depending on the type of process and level of maturity of the company, these are the areas noted for their value and effectiveness with suppliers:

1. *Cost reduction*—Honda Purchasing uses target costs for each component; a target cost includes a calculation of the supplier's projected material, labor, overhead, and profit. Comparison of actual run costs to the projected costs allows both Honda and the supplier to monitor productivity and quality performance, and frequently has resulted in cost-reduction opportunities that are shared with the supplier.

2. *Quality improvement*—Since Honda's pioneering U.S. motorcycle production start-up, followed in short order by a full range of vehicles, quality performance has improved significantly, especially at the supply base. Although the Honda manufacturing plants conduct no incoming inspections, quality across all commodities continues to be a challenge. The enterprise-wide goal is zero defects, an objective that can only be realized when all enterprise partners—second-, third-, and even fourth-tier producers—are expert at a variety of quality processes.

3. *Product research and development*—Unfortunately, traditional purchasing and R & D practice keeps an arm's-length relationship between these two powerful functions. At Honda, Purchasing encourages suppliers to rethink design details; suppliers are expected to "lead the way" in new process and product technologies.

4. *Teaching self-reliance*—Even when all supplier partners in Honda's extended enterprise have reached an assured level of self-reliance, the industry will continue to serve up new challenges. Honda's objective, however, is to work with suppliers whose process capabilities and associates are so strong and mature that they can handle any unforeseen problem that appears. What the company does not want to engender is a big company/parent-child relationship. Growth is the goal.

The areas of associate development, contributions to advancing the field of purchasing, and supplier alliance work were cited as important benchmarks in Honda's journey. Honda's purchasing practices and supplier involvement in new product design, as well as sourcing and production, are important because of the advances that Honda brings to the automotive industry in these crucial areas that impact quality, speed, and costs. Winners of the Medal of Excellence set new standards. They raise the bar within their industry and their profession.

Purchasing is NOT a Support Function

Traditional purchasing practices indicate less than keystone significance of the purchasing function. Organization structures are limited, job rotations may be infrequent or never, salaries do not reflect a high level of professionalism, and other indicators show procurement as a secondary track to the executive office. At Honda, however, just as many top executives have risen through racing programs and all understand and love the workings of an engine, Purchasing also has a history of drawing future top executives through its doors. Although the HAM supply base numbers over 400 companies, and approximately the same number of purchasing associates maintain and develop that extended enterprise, several hundred other associated functions are frequently staffed by former purchasing pros such as Jackie Hammonds, Honda quality guru. Quality, manufacturing, and engineering associates also work with suppliers, elbow to elbow with Purchasing people.

Purchasing at Honda encompasses the selection, development, and sourcing of over 6,000 parts from more than 400 U.S. suppliers, most of whom are located within 3 hours of the Marysville complex. The Purchasing organization includes over 400 associates who report to a vice president of purchasing who answers directly to the HAM president. Honda's flat organization structure has few layers, few titles, few managers. The goal is to keep bureaucracy (multilayered barriers) out.

Days are communication- and meeting-intensive, as groups of associates come in and out of team meetings. Faxes, e-mail, and telephones run 24 hours a day. The company's corporate travel schedule keeps purchasing associates on the road one day per week, on average. Suppliers and potential suppliers visit daily, as do many other groups of benchmarking teams, even managers from rival car companies.

Honda of America Purchasing scope

Purchased materials account for over $7 billion per year of MRO (maintenance and repair operations), original equipment, construction, services, components, and assemblies, broken into commodity groupings that either supply items for direct assembly into vehicles, production support items and services, or machines and equipment, and facilities construction.

Of the twelve tasks of HAM Purchasing shown in Figure 5.1 below, three points (numbers 10, 11, and 12) are the focus of BP and

Figure 5.1   Functions of Purchasing

Functions of Purchasing

1. Meet the needs of the company and department as they relate to new model development; identify and realize new technology; and understand the company's expansion plans.

2. Establish the purchasing plan, quantity of supply, and the target cost (budget).

3. Negotiate the prices for all items to be purchased.

4. Determine the maker layout according to the items to be purchased.

5. Decide the final cost of all items.

6. Finalize the agreement for purchase of all items.

7. Place the purchase order for all items from prototype to mass production, including tooling and related production items.

8. Expedite the delivery or installation and completion of items to the operation schedule.

9. Meet and maintain the budget targets.

10. Follow the performance of each supplier.

11. Countermeasure problems quickly as they arise.

12. Provide overall supplier support.

Copyright Honda of America Mfg., Inc. 1990. Used with the permission of Honda of America Mfg.

other improvement activities. Purchasing associates responsible for specific commodities select, source, monitor performance, and monitor BP and other improvement activities for their suppliers.

Sourcing Policy at Honda

Honda Motors' goal is to develop and supply products that fulfill consumer needs. Because suppliers sell their parts and materials through Honda to its customers, sourcing policies are particularly important to purchasing associates, including BP personnel, who facilitate customer satisfaction. Honda purchases approximately 75 to 80 percent of a vehicle's total product cost, all of which must meet Honda quality specifications, including delivery times. Further, parts and raw materials must be acquired at worldwide competitive costs.

Two objectives have guided the development of Honda of America's global extended enterprise since the first suppliers signed on in 1979:

1. The establishment of a competitive and stable supply base;
2. The establishment of an effective, self-reliant purchasing framework.

BP and other supplier development activities are key drivers of the growth of a stable supply base.

The Supply Base

Decisions about where and from whom the company buys parts, about supplier performance requirements, and about supplier relationship development and communications all contribute to the leadership role purchasing continues to take in the company's operations. Purchasing at Honda not only qualifies and selects suppliers as an ongoing activity, but, since the supply base of over 400 companies is not in constant churn, Purchasing associates, with their supplier partners, become experts at that supplier's process as well as their products.

Self-reliant Purchasing Framework

In less than 20 years, the North American operations of HAM have moved from dependence on Japan for product design and 90 percent of parts content to self-reliance in the areas of design, sourcing, and supplier development for over 90 percent of assembly parts, in addition to vehicle assembly and engine production.

Supplier selection and ongoing relationship building has always been formed by four guidelines:

1. Purchase where the company produces.

    Purchasing all parts, raw materials, components, and assemblies, from mature, stable suppliers in the extended enterprise, allows the company to focus on growth and quality, without the distraction of transoceanic logistics challenges and internal cultural or monetary exchange issues. By developing strong, localized networks, the company has insulated the supply base from many, but not all, external disruptive forces. Trade restrictions, currency disasters, political instability—all these elements preclude the purist operation of lean, just-in-time operations with minimum pipeline inventories.

2. Purchase on a competitive basis.

    The majority of Honda of America parts are single sourced, with only one set of tooling for each part. However, many parts are "competitively sourced." A steering wheel, for example, may be sourced to one supplier for the Accord and to another supplier for the Civic. Each supplier is capable of producing both models, and each would like to win a larger part of Honda's business. In fact, when new models are introduced, the supplier that is doing the best overall job in quality, cost, delivery, and technology wins the business.

3. Purchase worldwide.

Eight to ten percent of purchases for North America are globally sourced. The remainder has been localized over the last 15 years.

4. Develop strong, long-term supplier relationships.

Leveraged supplier methods, traditional "Buy/Sell" or "Bid/Quote" deals, and purchased price variance decision-making do not build a long-term relationship and will not strengthen the extended enterprise. Big dreams, like the vision of becoming a global producer that Mr. Honda held even as he struggled with initial engine development, need big visions and a long-term perspective that values relationship-building and trust.

Former HAM president, Hiroyuki Yoshino, had bad news to report to the eight Honda Motors board members. Profitability had fallen short of previous projections. But after Mr. Yoshino gave his report, nobody raised a voice or reacted with threatening displays of anger. A new member of HAM Senior Management attending his first board meeting was surprised. This was not what he would have expected in most traditional corporations. He expected the directors to "look for blood" and asked CEO Kume why the reaction was so calm.

"You must understand so that you use this (approach) in your management style. What do you think would happen next time if the associate was pounced on when admitting to an error? Next time he would shade the truth a little, or misrepresent the facts. We have to have the facts; nobody should ever be afraid to come to you."

How unlike the street-fighting most production and purchasing pros learned in their first days on the job. Managers shoot the bearer of bad news, so the lesson they teach employees is: If you can't fix the problem, hide it!

Excellent Suppliers Need Excellent Customers

> *"The reality is that most companies are too busy doing 'market research' to learn from their customers and too busy setting 'quality standards' for suppliers to learn from them."*
>
> Michael Schrage,
> *Los Angeles Times* industry analyst

Long-term relationships require dedication and trust, skills that take years to develop and nurture. Partnering for the extended enterprise is not a one-sided exercise. So Honda continues to work hard demonstrating to both associates and suppliers how The Honda Way works in practice. Being a good customer takes practice too; becoming a world-class customer is difficult work. If a customer chooses to work on only half the partnership—supplier development, for example, or certification—the partnering results will be, predictably, limited.

There are four proven action steps to becoming a world-class customer:

1. *Ask them.* Listen for clear signals. World-class customers practice listening and frequently survey suppliers to learn how they are doing as a customer.

2. *Tell them.* Share important information. Honda shares designs, schedules, cost date, and special topic information with suppliers. Evaluate all paperwork routinely initiated or processed by purchasing for usefulness.

3. *Invite them.* Invest in relationships. Supplier councils, supplier recognition days, joint benchmarking forums, and other open-door activities build trust.

4. *Work with them.* Work together. When the distinctions between customer and supplier partners begin to blur, customer-supplier partnership teams take on the appearance of a virtual company, a new organization formed with elements of all contributing partners. Most BP participants are shocked by the Honda associates' willingness, from the first day on the job, to pitch in and share the burden.

HONDA'S BIGGEST ASSET IS ITS ASSOCIATES

All the tactical tools Honda employs to drive its world-class procurement system are based on people—their training, their values, and their communication systems. Not every automaker or supplier can point to the same ideal purchasing associate profile; indeed, selection of good candidates is only the first step to bringing out the best skills in each new hire.

Dave Curry, purchasing administrator in charge of college recruiting, spends 18 weeks every year on the road, talking to college students and other groups, actively recruiting new additions to Purchasing. "There is not one ideal candidate," he says, "although the majority of the people are type-A personalities." The hiring process is intended to explore and define the candidate's value system, communication skills, and attitudes toward work and learning. "We don't get real technical during the interview," he says. "If they have demonstrated they can get through the college program with a decent grade-point average, then we look for attitude and ability to learn new ways." The majority have purchasing degrees.

Screening does not include personality or intelligence tests. "We sit down and talk with them." Interviewers are looking for the thought process. They might ask about favorite and least favorite classes, but their questions about the candidate's experience with team assignments and the role he or she took on the team are very important, because how the candidate reacts to new team challenges and time required above a straight eight-hour day determines how successful the associate will be in Honda's very demanding work environment.

"We don't want them to salute and move over," continues Curry, "if we have to ask them to drop a special project and move to another. We are hoping that although they look forward to new challenges, they will suggest ways to see the first project through, showing us a sense of ownership and responsibility toward the team. Then, we give them a situation in which they need to show a sense of urgency." For example, an associate responsible for buying tires gets a call at 3:00 on Friday afternoon. A piece of equipment has broken down and Monday's delivery is in doubt, a line-down situation. The candidate's response demonstrates thought processes and an ability to reach out and ask a team of suppliers, engineers, or even managers for help.

"We go all over the country looking for the best people, and we bring them and make them better," says Curry.

Every associate Honda hires into purchasing spends two weeks on the production floor, learning the process, the parts, the people, and the products. All 12,000 associates start out with philosophy training, what Curry says "separates us from everybody else." Next is a half day of safety and hazardous material training for everyone, because in the manufacturing facilities there is not a single associate who does not go out to the production floor.

Twenty or thirty years ago, job descriptions for purchasing buyers and planners might have required candidates to have a business background and to be good negotiators. Seldom were candidates expected, however, to understand manufacturing or even to be comfortable walking on the production floor. All that has changed, as the new purchasing professional will, as before, have a solid business sense, but now may have an engineering degree or experience in manufacturing or training as well.

Which college majors supply the best candidates? Purchasing degrees count, but so do graduates who started out in engineering and later transferred to business.

"We are brutally honest," adds Curry.

Honda is not for everybody. Hiring managers emphasize that they don't want to make a mistake, because the decision is a long-term one. For example, an open-office atmosphere (no cubicles, no corner offices, no rank signaled by the employee's office size or parking space) does not work well for everyone. Associates must be able to tune out the noise of other conversations; they must be skilled at working with high-stress, high-responsibility tasks, from the first day. Titles change infrequently, although day-to-day responsibilities and challenges are constantly growing, frequently due to the associate's initiative.

As quickly as new hires can handle their responsibilities, they get more, along with more authority and pay. Managers oversee from 20 to 80 associates. Total compensation packages for a first-year hire are 20 percent above the general North American average for purchasing, well in competitive range with other organizations looking for these same hires.

All new hires are scheduled for a rotation on the production floor, after which they are assigned a mentor. Then things start to happen very quickly, as the associate develops a training needs analysis with his or her new supervisor and, together, they set up a training schedule. Course selections for the first three months might include computer classes, how to lead meetings, or quality training, all of which prepare the new associate to work with suppliers.

Job rotations are a major contributor to Honda's associate development program. Recent high growth and expansion have limited the company's ability to keep employees for the preferred three years in specific jobs. The current average is approximately two years. If an associate has experienced one or two full model changes in his or her first position, the process of starting up a new model and closing out an old one constitutes a lifetime of rapid learning. As model changes for Accords, Civics, Acuras, minivans, and other introductions accelerate, associates will eventually experience multiple, parallel changeovers.

Other tools used by HAM Purchasing and its suppliers include a world-class production scheduling and network control system recently developed to serve the entire 400-supplier network. But it is Honda's quality and supplier development programs, especially its BP Program, that transform the procurement role from a supplier acquisition and monitoring approach, to a proactive, aggressive, supplier improvement powerhouse that Honda believes will take the entire auto industry from Six Sigma performance—98 percent of the parts delivered perfect and on time—to zero defects, all parts, all the time.

Clearly, Honda's leveraging of purchasing skills contributes significantly to the success of its extended enterprise. Purchasing associates' ability to understand the challenge of supplier relationships, to quickly evaluate supplier requirements and capabilities relative to Honda production plans, and to work with suppliers to achieve new goals differentiates these members of the extended enterprise from the traditional purchasing professional. It takes a flexible, superb communicator who "finds his job as it appears" to develop a successful network. The integration of dozens of supplier managers and employees only adds to the complexity of this very challenging, high-adrenalin, high-rewards job.

THE CHALLENGE

If only strong networks of high-performing customers and suppliers will dominate the next century's competitors, then why doesn't every company use its purchasing department to gain strategic competitive advantage? Almost none do.

Why do companies use purchasing only as a tactical weapon to fix yesterday's problem, a line-item adjustment to the income statement, a lever over suppliers? Marketing is not the only strategic means to a company's success. Honda's commitment to its purchasing organization, including supplier support and development, extends through good times and bad. Even in tough economic times, the allocations to bring on new purchasing associates that fuel the company's growth have always retained priority, even under tight budgets.

6

The Supplier's Role in the New Partnership

Becoming the Supplier of Choice

INTRODUCTION

Partnerships work best with two committed, strong partners. The supplier's responsibility in the alliance is to first become the supplier of choice, and second, to maintain a superior level of quality and delivery performance. Although big customers can make suppliers' work hell, they can also, by communicating well and often with their partners, make it easier for suppliers to achieve competitive performance levels. Further, second-, third-, and even fourth-tier companies contribute to overall cost reduction goals; if their operations are crisis-driven, they become more expensive manufacturing partners. The challenge for suppliers, therefore, is to become the supplier of choice. The challenge for customers is to select partners well and manage a productive relationship.

EVERY CUSTOMER'S DREAM

How does a supplier become the supplier of choice? By providing what all customers want from their suppliers: comfort, consistency, and respect. Customers want predictably high quality in product and delivery. They are happy to not be visited periodically by salespeople if they know that their requirements are understood and will be delivered as promised. Sounds simple enough, but clearly not all suppliers adopt best practices that enable them to deliver consistently high-quality products.

When suppliers step up to the excellence challenge—free of coercion and leveraging—their business skyrockets. In the plastics industry, for example, thousands of small suppliers make payroll with barely acceptable quality; yet those producers who, like Nypro in Clinton, Massachusetts, envision a partnership with their customers and participate in their design process from end to end, stand high above their competition. In the electronics industry, where every backyard garage can house a small board shop, a few visionaries, such as President Ko Nishimura of Solectron and CEO Jack Calderon of EFTC, have deliberately positioned their companies to be first-tier, world-class suppliers in an industry populated with second- and third-tier shops. Solectron's phenomenal growth over the past ten years has reinforced this first-tier vision, even when the company was racing to fill its first customer orders.

Some companies take a paper-intensive planning approach to their business, bolstering a weak relationship with customers and a less than secure retention rate with pounds of cascading business plans, quarterly reports, and daily sales quotas. The latest in a long series of revisions to their plans will, of course, merely reflect the latest in a long series of stated objectives—make more money, double the sales, cut costs. But where does all this master's degree complexity take supplier executives who buy into the strategy? These suppliers are focusing their enormous energies and their associates' creativity and power on the wrong thing. Simple is better. Complexity is no substitute for building a solid process whose end result will inevitably be better products and happier, growing customers. If you build it (the process), they (the profits) will come.

BP exemplifies the right balance in a customer/supplier focus that does not, for example, declare cost-down as its primary target. The target, which inevitably feeds cost reductions in its improved productivity, is to create improvement, to identify and eliminate waste. If a supplier does that properly and well, the money will come; if a supplier understands its customer and offers a lean, productive process, the business will come.

It's Not Better Crisis Management

Small- and medium-sized suppliers, like most of Honda's 350-member global extended enterprise, have finite energies to dedicate to planning and execution versus expediting and crisis management. Suppliers have a choice of either throwing their powerful but limited energies into resolving screwups or aggressively pursuing the creation of a positive, lasting goal, such as a better reputation, more money, or a safer competitive position. Honda supplier Parker Hannifin, for example, takes exactly this approach to excellence; their process capabilities and management philosophies guarantee repeat business.

Crisis management takes a heavy toll on customer/supplier partnerships. When customers award a particular supplier with their business and then are hit with small performance issues (manpower shortages, a forgotten small component part order, or missing welding rods, all of which can shut down their partner's line), they remember. The customers' expectation when they place the order is that their supplier partner has the ability and the urgency to solve these small challenges themselves, and that they will find a solution on their own.

Honda's role as a major customer is not to cripple its suppliers by interfering with the strengthening of the suppliers' capabilities. Although they sometimes become involved in last-minute problems, the strategy of building an extended enterprise of hundreds of self-reliant suppliers cannot move forward with dependent, crisis-driven partners. For Honda and most major producers' engineering and problem-solving resources, there is no problem too big but they prefer not to rush in. Crisis management and precrisis process improvement eliminates the adrenalin rush of line shutdowns. Shortage control and process problems properly belong to the real experts, the suppliers whose success depends on mastering the challenge. This dedication to supplier self-reliance is simply another variation on Honda's "Go to the Spot" principle.

Suppliers Solving Supplier Problems—Taking Care of Business

Supplier self-reliance requires a nontraditional approach to organizing the purchasing function. Commodity teams, high-level partnering, dedicated new product and engineering expertise are structured directly into the new supply base management organization structure.

Because the role of purchasing is not to buy from salespeople, but rather to form alliances that bring value to the company, many world-class suppliers have made the move from salespeople to sales engineers, a change well-appreciated by customers who look to suppliers to participate in problem-solving initiatives primary to successful, repeated, fast new product launches. Sales engineers solve problems and form working, productive relationships with their customer partners. One of Honda's excellent Midwest stamping suppliers' sales engineers' role, for example, is to spend most of their time in the plant, not selling, but talking about issues that make the relationship and the communications better. The era of suppliers showing up at a customer's doorstep to complain about business problems—"We are losing business, our volumes are down, we can't take a price cut, etc., etc."—is well over for enlightened members of the extended enterprise.

Solectron's Bob Levallee, East Coast Development Manager, emphasizes this move to relationship building and problem solving above selling. Bob's approach to growing the business has always been to work at very high levels in the customer organization to frame a working partnership that defines ongoing communications and development needs. He employs no salespeople and fully expects that as design-in and other advanced technology issues take precedence over delivery and quality questions, the level of partnering activity in his organization can only rise.

HONDA EXPECTATIONS OF SUPPLIERS

Nothing clarifies the high expectations automotive producers like Honda have for their suppliers than Honda's annual Supplier Conference Awards. For one day each year, Honda invites all suppliers to recognize their contributions to the company's growth, to hear upcoming plans for new products and new plants, and to thank supplier associates for their continued improvement. Each year, supplier awards recognize those particular suppliers whose performance is zero defects in quality and delivery performance in various commodity groups. Other awards recognize "above-and-beyond" special project work.

Raising the Bar – Perfect Quality, Faster Introductions

Clear goals and metrics designed to track quality and delivery performance make it easy for customers and suppliers to focus on specific process improvements. Suppliers understand from the beginning of their relationship with Honda what expectations their customer has for quality performance, by commodity and by individual part number. Each year, quality goals tighten up while delivery performance, because of the cost of line-down situations and recovery planning, continues to call for 100 percent on-time (not early and not late) deliveries. Honda, like all the leading auto producers, is a demanding customer that expects its suppliers to continue to meet high performance standards, even as the company grows. It's a tough bill to fill, and one from which only one supplier has walked away.

Perfect Quality, Every Time

Suppliers who attended the Honda 1997 Supplier Conference were told to expect higher production levels and increased export production as Honda auto production in North America and South America was projected to reach 820,000 vehicles for the year. Vice President of Purchasing Cesar Penaherrera emphasized the suppliers' role in raising the bar: "HAM suppliers are setting a new standard in the industry. Last year, 122 suppliers had a perfect record for quality—zero rejects. In addition, 229 suppliers had a perfect record for delivery—100 percent on-time delivery."

Eighty-seven awards went to 70 companies, some of whom were winning for the first time, some of whom won more than one award. Bearse Manufacturing Co. of New Windsor, New York, one of HAM's original suppliers, has been furnishing Gold Wing motorcycle saddlebags and trunk bags for fifteen years; Bearse won an award for the sixth year in a row, the Delivery Performance Award.

Basic qualifications for supplier awards include:

- Quality—Be in the top 15 percent of commodity type as measured by quality rejects in ppm (parts per million), and meet the Delivery average
- Delivery—100 percent on-time delivery of all parts (none early, none late), and meet the Quality average
- Productivity—A supplier-initiated activity, which results in significant gains in productivity or efficiency
- Production Support—Raw material rejects of zero ppm and 100 percent on-time delivery

Despite these very encouraging statistics, associates were reminded of the previous year's still unmet and very aggressive target. In Quality, supplier-delivered parts quality the previous year averaged 312 rejects per million, slightly up from the previous year, and more than double the target of 150 ppm. With an ultimate goal of zero ppm, some suppliers would find themselves considerably challenged, but others attest to the possibility of attaining this high level of performance. One hundred twenty-two suppliers reached the zero ppm goal, and 240 producers, or 70 percent of the supply base, achieved the 150 ppm target.

The Certification Challenge

Added to the quality challenge, many automotive customers like Honda are requiring suppliers to provide Quality Systems conformance, such as ISO 9000 and ISO 14000. Although ISO requirements are generally described as quality documentation process control systems, rather than product or process improvement systems, the very disciplined approach required to gain certification guarantees a higher degree of quality focus in every organization that has attempted it.

The New Product Introduction Challenge

Finally, all industries, particularly electronics and automotive, have redesigned their new product introduction processes to launch new models more frequently, with massive design changes and a real need for expert supplier design input. But only those suppliers that have complete command of their production process can hope to participate meaningfully in the stream of upcoming new products. According to Penaherrera, supplier rejects spike during new model launch; in the automotive sector, late new model appearance at the showrooms cost market share.

Of Honda's 400 suppliers, 227 met the on-time delivery performance goal of 350 ppm; further, 229 had zero delivery ppm. The ten percent of suppliers who exceeded 1,000 ppm understand that with that level of performance, their customer will be uncompetitive and unhappy. They have been challenged to take control of their disappointing delivery performance.

Bad Process = Predictably Poor Quality

What are the causes of poor quality? Surprisingly, they are not always production or process problems. Seventy percent of the problems that affect the production lines are a result of label errors. These "administrative defects" represent a strong cause of potential downtime in plants. Most lean manufacturers operating in a tightly scheduled JIT environment have no time to recover if mislabeled parts reach the assembly lines. Although EDI transactions replacing early supply chain software help speed communications, if parts in inventory or in process are mislabeled, they are basically lost. There is no substitute for robust, consistently maintained material movement processes.

Prototypes and Tooling in New Product Gains

In addition to meeting Honda's tough quality targets, suppliers must participate in their customer's aggressive new product introduction goals by shortening prototype leadtimes—meeting all trial and test schedules—and by improving prototype quality levels. Prototype samples' process and material characteristics should simulate mass production results as much as possible because that will allow earlier verification of functionality and design. In the design and planning area, suppliers continue to be asked to shorten their production tooling leadtime; as more new tools are built domestically, there will be less time to respond to design changes. The clock is ticking, and supplier expertise, encouraged by their associates' participation in the process, makes a difference.

How to Become the Supplier of Choice

With such aggressive demands for supplier quality performance, as well as fast new product introductions, small- and medium-sized suppliers are especially challenged to understand where to focus their attention. When Honda evaluates suppliers, the template they use, QCDDM (quality, cost, delivery, development speed, and management attitude), covers most operating issues. Among these five performance elements, management attitude reigns as the overwhelming deal-breaker. It's about alignment. Although management's attitude must not exactly mirror its customer's, both parties must feel that "they are moving in the same direction," that they share similar goals in quality and continuous improvement, and they need to demonstrate respect for the individual. Similar to Bob Levallee's Solectron partnering strategy, these key partnering performance elements are evaluated in very high-level management discussions.

Honda looks for performance capabilities and management attitude, or alignment, as well as specific equipment and technology capabilities. Potential partners must demonstrate a keen awareness and leadership in new technologies. Finally, when all these elements, especially the management attitude factor, check out, a procurement team of purchasing, engineering, and possibly R & D conducts a thorough site visit.

Fifty Years of Partnering History and Growth

The careful supplier evaluation and selection methods that look at suppliers developmentally, measuring their capacity for incremental growth, take time and careful thought. This approach has worked successfully with all but approximately 12 suppliers. Of those 12 who did not continue, most opted out of improving their quality to the customer-required levels. In almost 50 years of global growth, these numbers illustrate Honda's purposeful selection of suppliers, not just for their actual proven performance, but also for their excellence and growth potential. Of the Honda motorcycle suppliers who launched Mr. Honda's auto business, 95 percent are still suppliers.

LEVERAGE BP TO BECOME THE SUPPLIER OF CHOICE, MAKE THE COMMITMENT

BP associates illustrate the concept of taking on the improvement challenge with the breakfast story of the chicken and the pig. Which animal is more valued and more dedicated to its job at the breakfast table? The pig is, of course, because although the chicken will still be there, supplying eggs every day, the pig, supplying bacon and ham, is "committed"! Signing up for any continuous improvement program requires true commitment.

How M & M Became the Supplier of Choice

When M & M Engineering took on a chunk of Honda's instrument panel business, their process capabilities were already well-proven. As a 15-year supplier to Honda and other carmakers, they were accustomed to big orders from big, demanding customers. And they are masters of technology challenges. Over the company's 20-year history, this family-founded and family-run business has managed to instill specific areas of expertise in each of the founding brothers. John is the president and oversees general business operations. Dave is, among other talents, a mold and metals expert, and Mike is the company's third technology expert.

Honda Purchasing believes there isn't another company like M & M in the world. While still in high school, founder John's father helped start him out by "acquiring" a steel airport hanger. Together they unbolted the structure and reassembled it at their site in Indiana. From the first day, this supplier was determined to be special—world-class and innovative. John took a personal interest in issues such as housekeeping and plant pride.

Instrument Panels

Honda had previously sourced the instrument pipe on which the instrument panel attaches—a very complicated assembly with critical dimensions—to a transplant company. But BP guru Terry Maruo wanted to localize the part and the technology, and in 1996 he asked M & M to take on the Civic instrument panel.

Although M & M had provided excellent stampings for Honda, the IP (instrument panel) was new technology for the company. Honda Purchasing admits to having failed to stay on top of the start-up, and three months before mass production, M & M's weld line had not even been completed. The technology behind these instrument panels was not easily mastered, and when one of M & M's own second-tier supplier's delivery problems damaged M & M's performance, their reaction was immediate and comprehensive.

M & M sent a plane, with one of the brothers on board, to pick up their supplier's engineer; over the weekend, together they evaluated the situation and started countermeasures. M & M was willing and capable of doing whatever it took—airplanes, boats, or trains, and eventually several million dollars of new equipment investment—to beat the problem. M & M's unquestioning and unhesitating problem-solving response marked their alliance with Honda.

The time for truth telling came quickly, as Honda Purchasing associates approached management. "We've made a horrible mistake. Our supplier is not ready, and we cannot make this part for the money we thought." M & M's president's response, "I cannot put a dollar amount on my reputation," guaranteed that between the two partners, customer and supplier, they would never shut down Honda's assembly line.

Honda had already invested $3 million to $4 million in equipment, but that was not enough. Without hesitation, M & M spent another $8 million. Honda BP associates spent three months on site, battling process issues.

Six months later, M & M, having mastered Instrument Panel (IP) technology, took on three other Big Three instrument panel lines. The failure, like most BP challenges, became a benefit for other industry competitors.

This was not the first time M & M had broken new ground. Back in 1990, M & M conducted its first BP activities with Honda. HAM purchasing associate Tom Chickerella remembers their first efforts. Four BP associates from Marysville converged on M & M. They planned to improve productivity by using available equipment, keeping the investment low. Their expectation was to build confidence as they taught BP techniques to key supplier personnel.

But Chickerella remembers that after about two and one-half years of BP activities, although results were good (in one case, for example, a manpower redistribution from ten to eight people), their work "was not having a really big impact. Eventually, we decided that if we really wanted to have impact, we had to do it *before* equipment installation or *before* new model introductions."

Taking the process back, closer to the new product planning processes, broke new ground. "It was the first time we pushed BP back upstream. We looked at what type of tooling was used and why designs were completed in certain ways, and we even examined Honda specifications. We looked at how raw material was laid out and how raw material was stamped from a sheet to get us maximum utilization. We questioned how the material would feed and what the quality and waste levels would be. And we discovered," much to Honda's BP experts' delight, "that there was little risk for either Honda or its supplier if we made changes further up in the BP flow."

BP Phase I looks at "soft" issues, like die change time reduction, COP and material flow, and areas for layout improvements. BP Phase II, however, addresses capital equipment issues, as well as material specification and material usage.

Among various impact target areas, goals were set for both hard and soft issues—raw material utilization, for example, and offal usage. (Offal is scrap metal resulting from a cutting process.) Other goals covered cost of quality, space utilization, and tooling improvements.

Figure 6.1　Phase 2 BP Example

Phase 2 BP Example

Before

| BLANK SIZE: | $1.6 \times 1076 \times 609$ |
| INPUT WEIGHT: | 8.2423 Kg |

After

| BLANK SIZE: | $1.6 \times 1219 \times 445$ |
| INPUT WEIGHT: | 6.8132 Kg |

Other M & M Projects

For example, M & M and Honda BP associates redesigned a weld line that produced the mid-floor Accord cross members. Immediate cost savings came from the reduction of operators from 4 to 2, with an increase in productivity from 140 pieces per hour to 160.

Another welding improvement reduced costs on the Accord Wagon. The rear seat center pivot, a bracket welded onto the floor, offered another big savings opportunity. When supplier associates proposed a new welder, BP team members suggested reuse of an existing welder by adding a fixture to an older machine at a cost of $5,825. Both operations had previously run at rates of 135 pieces per hour; after the modification, the line ran to a two-step process, one at 95 pieces per hour, another at 240.

M & M had a four-door and a five-door welder. Chickerella remembers that although he is not a trained welding expert, as a BP team member he looks for equipment duplication. He realized that there might be a way to combine the two welders, using some quick-change fixturing that would minimize or eliminate the investment. M & M asked their weld equipment designers to develop the solution. The result was a per piece cost reduction of 6.9%, totaling $144,000 savings for the rear floor upper stiffener, a component that appears on four-door Accord Sedans and Wagons.

A bit of cannibalizing worked to retrofit old M & M welders to support the new Honda model. The problem was to keep the new line going while running the old model. M & M reutilized existing equipment with a common jig and other fixes. The equipment is owned by the customer, but M & M stepped in as welding equipment experts and made use of expertise that was not being tapped. The tab? Cost avoidance of $1.6 million, an agility success story.

BP idea tracking generated two pages of ideas that contributed to a series of improvements on the exhaust silencer mount hanger bracket.

BP team members started looking at the weld line and four stamping presses, asking why there were four separate processes.

Team members realized this kind of change could only be made early in the design cycle, back in development; they combined flange and restrike operations into one die. With a larger press, the operators would orient two dies in a different direction, which took the process down to two dies and a secondary blanking operation. The process change dropped machines from four to one; tooling impact was cut $16,344, but the big savings came in the individual part cost, which dropped over 50 percent. Overall program cost savings totaled $414,180 on the silencer bracket, but, says Chickerella, additional savings appeared from the improved process flow.

M & M had previously run the door hinge stiffener on a tandem line on four big presses, but they discovered that by getting very creative they could cut costs significantly. They brought in an old transfer press and reworked it to combine operations and added a robotic sealer, which dropped the number of operators for this process from nine to four. This change came about because team members simply studied the line, "at the spot."

The rear seatbelt anchor, a welded part, had been run on tandem lines. By observing and redesigning the flow, BP members moved the operation to run on two larger presses with three secondary operations, a better and more flexible use of equipment that resulted in savings of associates, from eight down to six.

"Running Down the Tab"

Eleven similar BP improvements generated piece part cost savings of $84,646 for parts such as door hinges, seat belt anchors, a support shelf, and the silencer bracket. All of these incremental improvements came about as associates studied, measured, and re-designed a process that was working adequately, but was not lean.

Raw Material

Additional savings appeared in the raw material area, as team members redesigned material utilization to cut scrap. Five parts, for example, in which the team proposed different steel specifications, a design normally made very early in the design/purchasing stage, produced similar materials savings.

The BP team looked at how the shark fin blank was processed. First the die was designed in-house, mounted on a pallet, and sent from HAM to an outside blanking company that proceeded to make the raw material into a blank, which they shipped to M & M. The process ran for the 1990 Accord. The BP team investigated all the parts and found one big piece of offal that seemed to offer savings opportunities if it could be designed correctly. Despite the fact that their solution required special dies to modify the Honda dies that would make the blank from this piece, and the addition of another processor, the overall program for the model's four-year life of the '94 Accord turned out to be, Chickerella says, "one of our biggest runners. We doubled the project goal! We could not have done this project on our own. You need the OEM to work with you. We had always some kind of offal blank material that could be used by suppliers. We just had to find a smarter way." Continued attention to material utilization yielded more savings; on the four-door Accord, redesigning the process for ten parts improved steel coil utilization overall from 62 percent to 65 percent.

Working Smarter

Quality levels for 15 parts dropped to the single-digit range when M & M tackled the problem of missing nuts on critical parts. Knowing that this is one problem that cannot travel far into the final assembly line, M & M created a nut certification system on 27 part numbers by retrofitting 12 different welders to verify the presence of nuts. The system uses a sensor that determines when the tip of the welder moves down to do the weld if the nut is in place.

For 14 parts that were studied over a 6-month period, overall cost impact amounted to $6.10 per car, a savings that totaled $6.22 million over the 4-year production cycle. The savings were split 50/50 between Honda and M & M.

Lessons from M & M—"Not for the Faint of Heart!"

Why, BP proponents ask themselves, don't all suppliers, who are truly the technology experts, do programs like this on their own? Chickerella feels that outsiders have an advantage of walking into a plant with instant credibility and power and top management support. "This program is successful because it uses the suppliers' expertise. It takes a lot of resources, and it's not for the faint of heart." This type of BPII activity, because it involves equipment development, takes longer; Honda's BP team had to work with the company about six months to start the process.

With more new models, and the customer's growing need for flexibility in equipment to meet model change, growth, and capacity shifts, this form of BP takes a whole different mindset to reduce supplier investment as the variety in parts and processes grows.

Chickerella acknowledges his initial fear that because he did not know these procedures in detail, he could not take BP from molding, to stamping, and then on to welding. But he learned from the M & M projects that "you can have the same results as me if you have the right way of thinking. Look for duplication of investment, look for flexibility in the process, being able to run a station wagon part and a four-door part on the same machine."

World-Class Customers Helping Suppliers to Improve

It takes world-class customers to help suppliers reach world-class performance levels. Customers need to speak clearly and reasonably, and freqently, about their current and upcoming requirements. Honda suppliers, like any other, want their customer to speak clearly about its daily operating requirements.

Some suppliers need, or believe they need, no improvement assistance. Some suppliers simply want to be measured and rewarded, while most small- and medium-sized American suppliers appreciate resources made available by their customer, such as quality train-

---

Four Action Steps to Becoming a World-Class Customer

1. Ask them.
2. Tell them.
3. Invite them.
4. Work with them.

---

ing, small-business administrative assistance, health and safety counseling, and BP.

But to become the supplier of choice, suppliers need to work at getting what they need from their customers, and customers need to listen carefully to supplier issues. It's a matter of perfecting communications flow, and working at establishing the routine and the contact points in the system that facilitiate partnering communications. Good customer-supplier partnerships are marked by four action steps. World-class customers recognize that they need world-class suppliers. And suppliers can only become as good as their customers help them to become.

1. *Ask them.*

   Practice listening. Periodic supplier surveys track how suppliers evaluate a customer's performance in the critical communications area. Motorola's supplier surveys, for example, not only pinpoint areas that need improvement, but they also establish a baseline for ongoing partnership monitoring and evaluation.

2. *Tell them.*

   Once made, promises—whether to provide better schedule information or more frequent new product updates—must be kept.

3. *Invite them.*

   Suppliers like to see and understand the end use of their components. When customers invite suppliers to their plants, they are making them part of the process.

4. *Work with them.*

Customer/suppliers teams guarantee, as Hewlett Packard and other pioneers have discovered, that the best team wins.

Preparation for surveys, and following through, especially disposition of confidential data, is as important as the survey content.

Figure 6.2   Customer Survey

Customer Survey

Purpose: To identify areas of concern that, with improvement, can strengthen our supplier customer relationship.

You are asked to complete this survey on our performance as a customer.
Return it to:

_____   _____

_____   _____

_____

Instructions: Please circle responses and add comments.

Coding of responses:	For functions or activities shown:	
1. Unacceptable	PRCH= Purchasing In General	S/D = Support and Development
2. Needs improvement	CPG = Purchasing Procurement Group	LOGS = Logistics Department
3. Meets expectation	PPMD= Production Parts & Materials Dept.	ACCT = Accounting Department
4. Exceeds expectation	QLTY = Quality Departments	XXXX = Cross Out If Inapplicable
5. Exceptional (best you have seen)	R & D = Honda Research Of America	_____ = Write In

1. Do you trust the following contact points of this company?

PRCH	ACCT	CPG	PPMD	QLTY	R & D	LOGS
1 2 3 4 5	1 2 3 4 5	1 2 3 4 5	1 2 3 4 5	1 2 3 4 5	1 2 3 4 5	1 2 3 4 5

Comments:

2. Is communication in general clear and timely?

PRCH	CPG	PPMD	QLTY	R & D	_____	_____
1 2 3 4 5	1 2 3 4 5	1 2 3 4 5	1 2 3 4 5	1 2 3 4 5	1 2 3 4 5	1 2 3 4 5

Comments:

3. How well are quality expectations communicated?

PRCH	CPG	QLTY	R & D	_____	_____	_____
1 2 3 4 5	1 2 3 4 5	1 2 3 4 5	1 2 3 4 5	1 2 3 4 5	1 2 3 4 5	1 2 3 4 5

Comments:

4. How well does Honda collaborate in continuous improvement?

PRCH	ACCT	CPG	PPMD	QLTY	R & D	LOGS
1 2 3 4 5	1 2 3 4 5	1 2 3 4 5	1 2 3 4 5	1 2 3 4 5	1 2 3 4 5	1 2 3 4 5

Comments:

Where any opportunity for misuse of survey data exists, or where a supplier would be intimidated into answering less than truthfully, a third party should mail and collate results to protect respondents and guarantee honest responses.

Honda regularly surveys all its suppliers. Dave Curry, purchasing

---

5. How well are agreed payment terms met?

PRCH	ACCT	R & D	_____	_____	_____	_____
1 2 3 4 5	1 2 3 4 5	1 2 3 4 5	1 2 3 4 5	1 2 3 4 5	1 2 3 4 5	1 2 3 4 5

Comments:

6. How well do prices and terms reflect total costs to Honda, services provided, mutual improvement goals, and sharing of prosperity?

PRCH	R & D	_____	_____	_____	_____	_____
1 2 3 4 5	1 2 3 4 5	1 2 3 4 5	1 2 3 4 5	1 2 3 4 5	1 2 3 4 5	1 2 3 4 5

Comments:

7. How well does Honda collaborate on advanced product or process technology?

PRCH	CPG	R & D	_____	_____	_____	_____
1 2 3 4 5	1 2 3 4 5	1 2 3 4 5	1 2 3 4 5	1 2 3 4 5	1 2 3 4 5	1 2 3 4 5

Comments:

8. How does Honda compare overall with all other customers?

PRCH	ACCT	CPG	PPMD	QLTY	R & D	LOGS
1 2 3 4 5	1 2 3 4 5	1 2 3 4 5	1 2 3 4 5	1 2 3 4 5	1 2 3 4 5	1 2 3 4 5

Comments:

9. Please comment on your overall experience with Honda in the past year or two. Are we improving? At what rate?

10. What one or two changes would you most like to see Honda make that would enable increased benefits to both of us? In what areas would the greatest benefits be achieved (such as quality, cost, technical progress, dedicating of capacity to us, etc.)?

administrator, stresses the necessity of protecting supplier confidentiality, because without honest responses the customer will have no
valuable improvement opportunities. Honda's 1997 survey was
completed by all its suppliers; those companies that attached business cards to their questionnaire had their cards shredded to guarantee an unbiased reading. Only two Honda associates reviewed
the responses before they were consolidated.

Next, consolidated responses are taken to all senior management
in purchasing, plus the senior person in all the other groups that
were affected, for example, R & D or accounting. Managers receive
a summary page and individual comments. The last step, making a
commitment to respond, requires management to provide the vice
president of purchasing with any plans they have on how to address
supplier issues.

Finally, Honda sends a letter to all the suppliers, thanking them
for their participation and presenting the list of resulting actions
being undertaken by their customer. Feedback includes concerns
that the company rotates contact people too frequently and that
suppliers need more coordination between manufacturing and various R & D facilities.

Dozens of companies like M & M and Progressive Industries
have chosen to become the supplier of choice, not just for Honda,
but for other majors. They have learned that BP is a powerful tool
that draws on the strength of their customer and the expertise of
their associates to reap huge savings and better processes that will
continue to fuel growth. They know that better production
processes yield leaner, more flexible, and inevitably higher quality
levels. And they have chosen to make the commitment.

7

BP, the Tool for Building the New Partnership

BP Vision and Mission Statement

Vision: Develop World-Class North American Suppliers

Mission: Contribute to the establishment of a competitive and stable supply base by supporting all aspects of supplier improvement from a foundation of trust, respect, professionalism, and ethics.

"Action without philosophy is a lethal weapon; philosophy without action is worthless."

Soichiro Honda

INTRODUCTION

Honda has learned from its rise to global dominance of several vehicle lines that a philosophy supported by simple and powerful improvement methods works in any environment. The integration of a few tools that focus on the power of people to understand problems and fix them, including the Deming Circle, the 3 A's, The Five Ps, root cause analysis, the Five Ss, visibility strategies, all under The Honda Way umbrella, make up the core of BP.

The test of any philosophy is the degree of commitment that members of an organization demonstrate, not by simple mental or verbal assent, but by real action. BP is Honda's demonstrated commitment to continuous improvement in its suppliers—The Honda Way philosophy in action. BP activities, as Honda calls its toolbox of continuous improvement methods, are simply an extension of Honda's own approach to internal manufacturing excellence. BP exemplifies Honda's partnering spirit with suppliers by offering them a hands-on, user-friendly focus for manufacturing improvement.

BP BEGINNINGS

Japan has been practicing continuous improvement assiduously since General Douglas MacArthur, post-World War II Japanese leaders, and W. Edwards Deming set about rebuilding the country's industrial base. BP had its start in Japan around 1979 at Honda Motors' Technical Support Group, which was, significantly, located in purchasing. With the spread of BP to North America, it has remained in the arms of purchasing, specifically in Marysville's

Support and Development Group. With each new company, each new project, the idea has grown as supplier companies reach into their own supply base and spread the good news about the power and simplicity of this approach. Successful implementations appear in a range of industries and products, in all commodities and disciplines, from plastics, to electronics, stampings, machined parts, seats, even raw materials.

Every revolutionary idea has its gurus—from Shewhart's studies at Bell Labs, to Deming's Circle, to Honda BP. Teruyuki Maruo, Senior Manager of Honda United Kingdom Purchasing, and Rick Mayo, manager of HAM's Supplier Development Group, tailored the methodology that they knew worked well in Japan to fit North American culture. Maruo knew the concept would work in North America, and the company needed a non-consultant-dependent, proven method to quickly establish a local network of high-quality suppliers.

What is BP?

The acronym BP stands for five improvement opportunities, all of which support Honda's manufacturing philosophy, as shown in Figure 7.1.

Why BP?

Like all Honda initiatives, BP is philosophy-driven and grounded in sound technical expertise. BP's creator gave us an effective product that could be marketed to the entire supply base at a time when small- and medium-sized producers needed a simple, hands-on continuous improvement approach. Maruo selected professionals from a wide range of technical and business backgrounds, such as engineering, production, and purchasing, to create a team of self-starters that reflected Honda's philosophies, yet was also independent enough to generate synergy at supplier sites.

The Honda IndyCar championship-winning engine is about the
same size as an Accord family sedan engine, yet produces more
than 800 horsepower.

Honda-powered Alex Zanardi of the Target/Chip Gnassi team won the 1997
CART IndyCar Driver's Championship, the second year in a row a Honda-
powered driver has won the top prize in American racing.

Soichiro Honda 1906–1991. The spirit and philosophy of Soichiro Honda continues to be present in Honda operations worldwide.

Soichiro Honda points with pride to the One Millionth car produced by Honda of America Manufacturing on April 8, 1988.

An Acura CL undergoes evaluation on a dynamometer at the Honda R&D Americas facilities in Ohio. The Acura CL is the first Japanese nameplate luxury car to be developed in the U.S.

A white body prototype of the all-new 1998 Accord Coupe is fabricated in the weld facilities of Honda R&D Americas in Ohio.

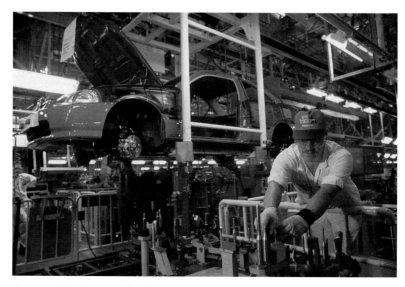

Automated equipment lifts the engine and drivetrain into a new Civic at the East Liberty Auto Plant in Ohio while a production associate prepares for the next model.

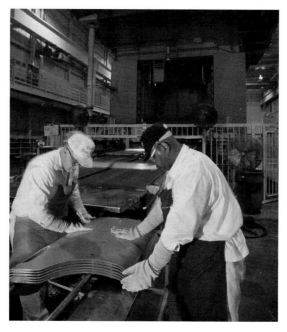

Two associates inspect a door panel stamped by one of the world's largest presses in the Marysville Auto Plant.

Honda's newest engine, a 200 horsepower V6, is made only at the Anna Engine Plant in Ohio.

A freshly painted Acura CL sport-luxury coupe emerges from the paint ovens at the East Liberty Auto Plant.

Cars go down the assembly line sideways at Honda's plant in Ontario, Canada.

The stylish new 1998 Accord Coupe was designed and developed by Honda R&D operations in the U.S. and is manufactured exclusively at the Marysville Auto Plant in Ohio for export around the world.

The Acura CL Coupe is the first Japanese luxury nameplate car to be manufactured in America.

Reflecting Honda's regional self-reliance strategy, the new Acura EL Sedan is manufactured exclusively at Honda's auto plant in Ontario for the Canadian market.

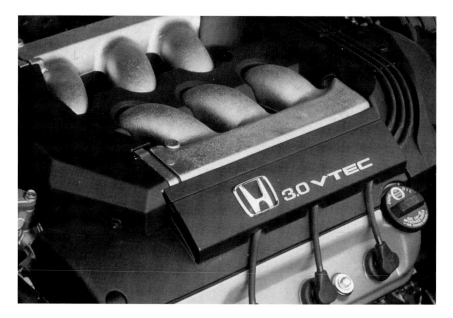

This all-new 3.0 liter V6 engine is made only at Honda's comprehensive engine and drivetrain plant in Anna, Ohio.

Figure 7.1 Honda BP

Best Position

Achieving the highest position of competitiveness in the global marketplace

For Honda to be the best, our suppliers must be the best.

Best Productivity

More output for less input (as measured by pieces per labor hour)

Best Product

A higher-quality product is the key to achieving competitiveness.
No sacrifice of the quality of the process to make productivity gains

Best Price

Reduction in the cost of manufacturing the part
Results from productivity gains

Best Partners

Synergy factor of knowledge transfer activity
Working together to develop a long-term relationship

Best Product		**Best Price**
+	**=**	**&**
Best Productivity		**Best Position**

There is a buffet of continuous improvement programs in industry today. Step up to the bar and make your selection: reengineering, TQM, teams, work flow analysis, MRP, finite scheduling, etc. Parker Hannifin, a successful Honda supplier that has made BP its own continuous improvement approach, had spent large sums of money on consultants to train its employees in lean production techniques. Several months and a few thousand dollars later, their expected result—a turnaround in corporate culture and performance—never appeared.

BP: A Bridge from Theory to Practice

What Parker Hannifin truly needed was an idea like BP to put philosophy into practice on the floor, a practical approach that would continually reinforce the new way of thinking. They needed to build a bridge from theory to practice. Fueled by a long-held desire for change, Parker used BP to bridge theory and practice. With each successful project, BP became more deeply embedded in Parker's culture.

How Difficult is BP?

Many suppliers frequently comment on BP activities' lack of highly complex, technical techniques. On their first encounter with the process, they are stunned by the *simplicity* of BP. "Basically, it's all common sense." Although the tools are indeed simple, there is no magic wand, and what *seems* to be the magic is—that there's no magic at all.

Team Makeup

A BP team includes one or two Honda associates and one or two supplier associates; these two groups work as a team to investigate and evaluate the areas and systems that can be improved at the supplier's facilities. Honda team members take on a training role as they show suppliers how to gather information, evaluate data, implement changes, and document the process and results.

The Goal

The goal—to create a highly productive, cost-effective manufacturing method—draws on the knowledge of production associates. These are "the experts," working in the targeted improvement areas, combined with the findings of the team. Immediate benefits flow to the work site and supplier associates as the team makes the plant more organized for production. Empowerment defines the team's partnering relationship with supplier associates, as everyone begins to understand that they are not assembling or making parts—*they are building a Honda.*

A secondary goal—to create a working partnership that produces mutual benefits for *all* partners—opens a new door for industry. In this partnership, each partner's responsibility includes bearing the shortcomings and debts of the other. Tom Kiely, an experienced Marysville BP pro, likens this shared truth-telling to "airing dirty laundry from both sides!" Honda's benefit in the short term is the improvement of productivity and efficiency that directly translates to the cost of purchased parts. The supplier partner's short-term benefit is the knowledge gained through the *systematic* learning that BP offers.

Long term, Honda wants a stronger, competitive supply base whose self-reliance ensures continuous improvement. Suppliers aim long term for overall competitive advantage, across all product lines, for all customers; the outcome of the BP experience for the supplier should be a reordering of the way the company as a whole does business.

And success is contagious. Each successive area or production line that experiences BP touches other departments—engineering, maintenance, quality, even the front office. As BP grows, it should systematically put itself out of business, leaving behind a company that exemplifies the BP philosophy in all its day-to-day operations.

BP TOOLS AND TECHNIQUES

What makes BP better? People...

Step one, people

They may be welding or assembly workers. They may work in quality, maintenance, or purchasing, but all the people on the Honda team are called *associates,* a tribute to the inherent importance in all improvement activities of respect for the people who make the product. The term *associate* delineates the difference between a "hireling" and a "stakeholder." A hireling has a job, but he is not respected for his contribution or his expertise. A stakeholder occupies an integral place in the business. Stakeholders are valued because their expertise benefits everyone.

Quick-hit kaizen programs rarely use a core team that asks for and listens to line associates for their improvement ideas. What a loss for the companies and industries struggling to raise their performance levels with inadequate methods, because it is *people*—Honda and its suppliers' strongest resource—that form the driver for sustained continuous improvement.

Release Associates' Creativity

The first step to bringing in and harvesting associates' ideas is to establish trust. Sad statements, such as "I've told people this idea before and nobody got back to me," signal opportunity among associates who are the true experts in the company. Their hands are usually the last ones to touch the part before the customer receives it, and, unfortunately, they are in most companies the most underutilized resource.

At TRW's Reynosa plant, BP team members used a BP Mailbox to gain supplier associate trust. They placed a small green box on the line, labeled it "Cual es tu idea?" (What is your idea?), and waited. Day after day the BP team performed its ritual walk over to the empty box. Each time, an English-speaking team member mimed his disappointment to line associates. When a single idea finally surfaced, the team seized it, investigated and implemented that idea with the associate who offered it.

The next day, more ideas appeared in the mailbox, and with each precious idea, trust grew. Each time an associate submitted an idea, she was really asking, "Can I trust you?" The BP team responded immediately with the engineering and maintenance departments to schedule and implement as many ideas as possible.

As trust grew, so did pride. Associates who were credited and saw their ideas implemented felt more pride in their work because they had ownership. They had an active improvement role. The people knew they were not "bodies" standing in the way of the team.

The power of growing self-esteem among associates is unstoppable. It costs nothing—no fees, no overtime, no bonuses—but it is the single wisest investment a company can make in its business. We call it empowerment. Empowerment breeds ownership. Ownership builds stronger associates. And stronger companies win. The cycle continues.

Step two, Plan Do Check Act (PDCA)

Everyone in business knows Dr. Edwards Deming's approach to quality improvement—Plan Do Check Act. Honda BP uses Deming's Circle in all its improvement activities for project management, problem solving, new projects and initiatives, and just about every serious effort any one associate or group of associates tackles. At the top level of project management, the entire BP approach follows Deming's PDCA format; in fact, *almost 70 percent of the project work falls into the Plan segment of PDCA.* The BP team thoroughly investigates to understand and document current situations on the line, before any improvements begin.

The *action* phase of the PDCA cycle—*Do*—by far the shortest segment of the project, includes simply implementing the Plan.

The *Check* phase is typically the weakest area in all continuous improvement efforts because companies fall into the trap of premature implementation, proceeding without checking results against the plan. During an extensive line/machine layout change implementation conducted at Parker Hannifin's Batesville, Mississippi, plant, as the BP team was checking results of process time improvements, they discovered that actual results fell slightly short of the goal. When team members revised machine performance, they uncovered opportunities for very minor improvements. The team approached Parker's engineering department with their solutions. Engineering's response, "You are babying the workers!" shocked everyone. It was clear that the philosophy of "tweaking," or *Checking,* a process to achieve its planned performance, had never been practiced.

Finally, the *Act* phase is the implementation naturally following the Check phase; action completes the cycle.

PDCA can also be used in the micro sense for very specific

Figure 7.2   The Deming Circle

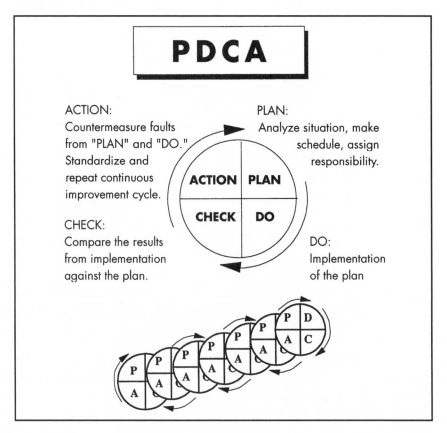

applications of individual implementation of ideas. Each idea is investigated thoroughly for its actual intent and feasibility before it is scheduled for implementation with the responsible party or department. Implementation responsibility can be assigned to anyone in the plant, either the person who generated the improvement idea, the BP team, or the associate ultimately responsible for implementation.

Step three, COPDS

Imagine this scene. On your next supermarket trip you find no grocery carts at the entrance. Inside, fresh produce is mixed with all other foods. Piles of cans and bottles and cardboard boxes block the aisles, a jumble of big and small containers. Bread, cereals, and canned goods are mixed with pet food.

If you were the store manager, how many people would you need to adequately serve customers? How fast could you process shoppers through your system? And would your patient customers happily return to the store, remembering the many pleasant hours they spent picking through piles of produce? Probably not!

Figure 7.3 COPDS

Phase 1 BP Techniques

∎ COPDS

		Results
C Clean up	**Clean appearance**	**Reduce Cost**
O Organize	**Logical order**	**Improved Quality**
P Pick up	**Eliminate unneeded items**	**Higher Morale**
D Discipline	**Maintain C.O.P.**	
S Safety	**Eliminate unsafe conditions**	**Improved Efficiency**

Copyright Honda of America Mfg. Reprinted with permission Honda of America Mfg.

A modern supermarket is a great illustration of throughput. A well-designed facility is completely customer focused. Its layout is logically formatted to speed the customer through the shopping process with minimum interference. You see clear, wide aisles. Labels are easily read and colorfully designed to stand out better among the thousands of choices. Signs posted above the aisles direct customer traffic to the right products. Usually, the only contact a customer has with store personnel is at the register, in response to the query "Paper or plastic?" *Manufacturing should be like that, visually clear, logically and simply flowed, with few questions, and no interruptions.*

BP contains a wonderful tool that makes manufacturing flow as simple and smooth as a good supermarket—*COPDS*—Clean up, Organize, Pick up, Discipline, and Safety. COPDS comes from the Five Ss, and it is one of the most powerful tools in the continuous improvement arena. COPDS forms the foundation for productivity improvement.

Clean Up

When companies ask employees to clean the plant only for customer visits, they are sending the wrong message. This approach tells the employees that they are not as important as the customer. Employees spend 50 percent of their waking hours in the workplace, so *Clean up* should be for them, as much as for the customer.

Clean up does not mean simply picking up a broom and sweep-

Figure 7.4   The Five S's

The Five S's	
Seiri	Proper arrangement
Seiton	Orderliness
Seiso	Cleanliness
Seiketsu	Picking up
Shitsuki	Discipline

ing. Anything that can be cleaned should be cleaned—machines, fixtures, part transfer systems. Equipment is an asset, a balance sheet investment in the business. *Clean up* is the right thing to do. Associates who clean and examine their equipment regularly get to know it better than associates who only touch their machines when they are operating, or who are completely dependent on other "experts" to maintain and monitor machines.

On one BP project conducted by a small Midwest die-casting facility, the model line, a zinc die-cast area, had three 1,800-ton machines that had not been cleaned since their installation. Zinc buildup on the machines was so thick that visitors could not determine what color they had been painted, a perfect COPDS opportunity. BP team members (Honda and the supplier) decided to not only clean the excess zinc and grime from the machines but also to apply a fresh coat of paint. A very thorough cleaning at the supplier revealed maintenance opportunities; cleaning will identify any hidden defects in equipment that can be fixed before they cause catastrophic breakdowns.

Cleaning a specific area or line also sends a strong message to supplier management. Management is embarrassed that their customer has begun to clean the equipment, and it sometimes takes patient teaching by the team to convince execs that the real benefit, after identification and correction of equipment defects, is increased performance.

Everyday life is filled with parallel examples of cleaning and maintenance opportunities. For example, if you always wash your car in an automatic car wash, you miss the opportunity to thoroughly inspect the exterior of your car. By washing and waxing the car by hand, you will readily discover scratches, dents, and loose trim. The same benefits come from cleaning equipment by hand; leaks become obvious, loose bolts and nuts can be replaced. *Clean up* forces associates to respond with an action because the hidden defect is now uncovered—one can no longer avoid seeing it—and it must be addressed.

Organize

"A place for everything and everything in its place" is a great maxim, but it is seldom practiced in manufacturing. Yet the benefits of organization are boundless. Marking floors to identify aisle lines and component/product locations, and putting product or components in their place, adds logic to the workstations. Label shelves of component parts with their correct part number and name. Another trick to guarantee an organized work area is to always size worktables to fit the work being performed, leaving no excess space to attract clutter.

Pick Up

Ask the question, "Does this item add value to the process?" If it does not, eliminate it. Start with the 24-Hour Rule: Any item that is not used or touched within 24 hours is not needed in the immediate area. Move these items to a storage area.

Discipline

Publish standards that define how an area should look. Emphasize the focus of COPDS. Ask the question, "Is this for the company itself, not just visitors?" You will know you are there when unscheduled downtime happens and associates automatically begin to restore the line to COP standard condition.

Safety

Honda BP gives correction of safety concerns the highest priority. Use safety awareness as a morale booster. You cannot shortcut safety in the process for the sake of productivity because you must protect your most valuable resources, the associates. Automation takes an important role in the drive to eliminate potentially unsafe operations. Consider automating the 3D's—the dirty, the difficult, and the dangerous.

Honda uses these criteria for automation evaluation as part of the company's overall approach to automation. The Automation Strategy requires a measured approach to balancing machines with

Figure 7.5   Honda Automation Strategy

Honda Automation Strategy

- Commitment to ergonomic processing—reaching, bending, turning, weight limitation
- Use of pneumatic, hydraulic assists

General rule:
Automate when the work is dirty, difficult, or potentially dangerous.

associates. Honda does not, for example, subscribe to a completely automated approach to its facilities, and the company expects suppliers will take the same measured strategy.

Step four, COP Strategies

BP uses another tool called COP Strategies to provide common examples or analogies that ease COPDS into action.

Strategy #1, The Wall Side Strategy

The Wall Side Strategy is a plant-wide approach to creating clear access around equipment for cleaning and maintenance. For example, think of the space behind your refrigerator. What does it look like now? Although no one would, of course, move the refrigerator into the middle of the kitchen, what about a $100,000 injection-molding press? What better way to identify hidden defects than by creating better access for regular maintenance?

Strategy #2, The Closet Strategy

The Closet Strategy removes seldom-used items from the workplace. Keep them out of the way, but close for quick retrieval, until they are needed. The "closet" must be maintained in an organized fashion. The Closet Strategy addresses the O (Organize) and P (Pick up) of COPDS.

Figure 7.6   COP Strategies

Phase 1 BP Techniques

- ## COP Strategies
  - Wall Side: Accessibility for
    Cleaning & Maintenance

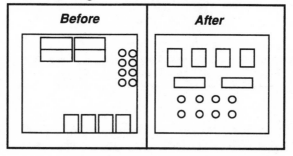

  - Closet: Better utilization of work space

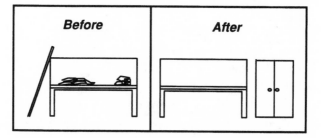

  - Kitchen: Needed items close at hand

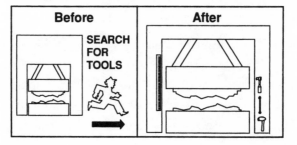

Strategy #3, The Kitchen Strategy

In any successful restaurant you will find an efficiently organized kitchen. Keeping frequently used tools or items close at hand is the focus of the Kitchen Strategy, because searching for tools is a waste of time that interrupts production flow, causes more wait time, and occasionally results in bad products when the wrong tool is substituted for the right one.

Die changes are a good opportunity to cut waste out of the process. BP teams frequently use videotape to study and improve die changes. On one die change project, team members used video to identify all the steps required by a changeover.

At first, press operators were wary, but they soon grew accustomed to the camera. As the team watched the video, they were amazed at the number of times the screen went blank. For whole minutes, no one appeared on screen during the die change. Was there a problem with the tape, or had the camera been turned off? The press operator was off searching the plant for tools to change the die, a perfect Kitchen Strategy opportunity. Team members relocated tools on a board next to the press, and changeover time dropped.

Figure 7.7 COP Strategies

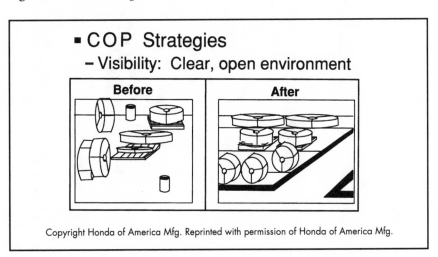

Copyright Honda of America Mfg. Reprinted with permission of Honda of America Mfg.

Strategy #4, Visibility Strategy

The fourth COP strategy is the Visibility Strategy, the total visual management system that organizes a facility so that day-to-day information and data is readily available to all. Each employee and manager can, at a glance, completely understand the situation, such as location of components or inventory, or production requirements for that day or shift. There are many effective visual tools. Production visual management boards are a good example.

At one large North American stamping supplier, the production supervisor kept the day's schedule in his back pocket. He was responsible for a sister facility four miles down the road, and when he could not be located quickly, associates did not know which jobs they were to run next, on which machines. The missing production supervisor added up to frustration for the associates and lost revenue for the supplier. The solution? The company installed a visual board at each facility, indicating the machines and priority of jobs to run that day.

Figure 7.8   Tool Board

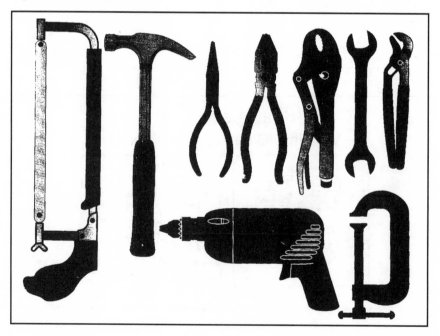

THE 3A'S

"A gold mine is not worked
inside a board room."

Terry Maruo

A mainstay of The Honda Way that is embodied in the BP process is "Being on the Spot," or the 3A's—see the actual place, view the actual parts, then analyze the actual situation.

The 3A's lead BP associates to ask, for example, where the project focus area is. Conduct the activity there because to mine the gold, the miner goes to where he hopes ore is buried. The production area is where all the skills, talents, ideas, and enthusiasm of workers come together for a quality product that is valuable to the customer and the end user. Although traditional management thinking allows employees to stay in the office, meeting with department heads and making assessments through reports, and very occasionally to visit the line to confirm report data, the BP methodology takes a more proactive view. Stay on the line, work with the experts, the line associates who add value, and occasionally check your on-the-spot analysis with data from the office.

Figure 7.9   The 3 A's

The 3A's

Go to the Actual Spot,
See the Actual Part,
Learn the Actual Situation.

A few years ago, Parker Hannifin's Jackson, Mississippi, plant assigned Joe Simms, a quality manager, full-time to the BP team, to learn the BP process. At BP War Room sessions, it had become clear that, although his statements were correct and followed policy and procedures, they were not supported by the actual situation on the floor. The team asked Simms if he would be willing to sit in the model area for one entire shift to learn the actual situation.

Simms reluctantly agreed, and the next morning he took a stool to the middle of the model line valve-brazing area, where he sat recording observations on a yellow legal pad. By lunchtime his legal pad was filled, and his enthusiasm for the power of the 3A's overwhelmed him. "I really did not know the actual situation on the floor," he said, as he produced pages and pages of notes, sketches, and numbers. He was converted, a BP believer grounded in reality.

THE SEVEN WASTES

The idea of MBWA (management by walking around) is very consistent with the 3A's. For a plant manager, MBWA means designating time to be in a specific area without being called in by a crisis. MBWA also means making the most of every opportunity to see the actual situation on the shop floor.

Tsuru Eyes

Tadamitsu Tsurouka, a Honda process engineer based in the Marysville auto plant Supplier Development Group, perfected the skill of identification of waste so that he could, after only a 20-minute plant tour, write pages on the facility's weaknesses. Typically, two to three weeks later, analysis confirmed all his observations. Honda BP group members called this remarkable skill "Tsuru eyes," and wished they too could develop it. Although Tsuru seemed to have a magical, intuitive gift of seeing what everyone else

Figure 7.10   Eliminate Waste! Does It Add Value?

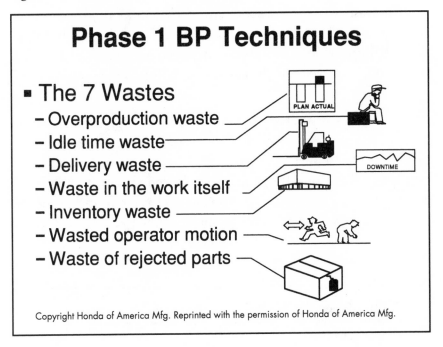

Phase 1 BP Techniques

- ## The 7 Wastes
  - Overproduction waste
  - Idle time waste
  - Delivery waste
  - Waste in the work itself
  - Inventory waste
  - Wasted operator motion
  - Waste of rejected parts

PLAN ACTUAL

DOWNTIME

Copyright Honda of America Mfg. Reprinted with the permission of Honda of America Mfg.

missed, BP practitioners believe that when they focus on the Seven Wastes, they continuously improve their ability to see the actual situation.

The Seven Wastes are those wastes that directly affect the productivity of the manufacturing process. The BP process focuses on identification and the elimination of these wastes.

Figure 7.11   Causes of Waste

Causes of Waste

- Inadequate processes
- Inadequate tools/equipment
- Inefficient layouts
- Lack of training
- Inadequate suppliers
- Lack of standardization
- Poor management decisions
- Mistakes by operator
- Inadequate scheduling

Waste #1, Overproduction

The waste of overproduction, producing more than is required, costs money and causes schedule problems. If a line has 7 jobs to run in a 24-hour period, and jobs 1 to 5 were overproduced, jobs 6 and 7 will not have enough schedule time for completion.

Waste #2, Idle Time

Idle time is waste built into the production process. Idle time usually accumulates when operators watch a machine run or take too much time fixturing a part while the machine remains idle. For example, during one BP project conducted at a machining supplier, one operator on a two-person line had a significant amount of idle time; for 18 seconds while the machine she operated performed

Figure 7.12   Over-Production Waste

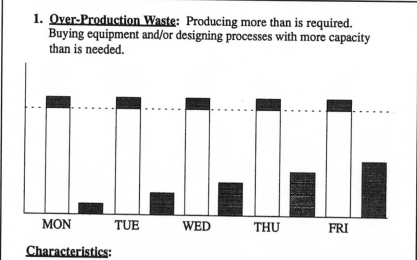

1. <u>Over-Production Waste</u>: Producing more than is required. Buying equipment and/or designing processes with more capacity than is needed.

MON   TUE   WED   THU   FRI

<u>Characteristics</u>:
- Excess inventory.
- Extra and/or oversized equipment.
- Plant cells/departments unbalanced.
- Pressure on production to raise utilization.
- "It's running good, so leave it running" syndrome.
- No urgency to attack quality problems.

a welding function, she was idle. A quick analysis showed the possibility of one operator performing two processes and maintaining the original output simply by utilizing the idle time.

When the BP team combined the processes, two things happened. Christine, the operator, initially complained that she was being loaded up with too much to do, and that there was no way she could match the original output. After team members convinced her to try and asked her for suggestions on how to rearrange the cell, Christine agreed to try the new process reluctantly and with great skepticism. After a brief learning curve, she began to not only match her original output, but she beat her best production rate! Later, Christine commented, "The day flies by, and we are making more than we used to!"

Warning! Do not use improved efficiencies to lay off associates! The operator displaced by the improved process was transferred to another line. The issue of trust is exercised most when dealing with reduced manpower in processes. The BP rule is "No layoffs due to BP." If empowerment of line associates is one of the major principles of improvement, and associates' ideas are paramount to the success of that improvement, what trust can be built if improvement signals the end of their employment? The company must be actively improving in all areas, including obtaining new business, to be truly competitive; improvement cannot come at the expense of the company's greatest asset.

Waste #3, Delivery

All delivery is waste because it adds cost without value. BP's goal with delivery waste is to reduce it to a minimum. One easy way to convert this technique to a tool is to measure part travel distance in feet, or to count the number of times a part is touched before completion.

One type of delivery waste seems to appear frequently. On one BP project, team members observing a line noticed that an operator had run out of component parts for the process. The line associate took a tub and walked about 15 steps to a large metal basket in the

Figure 7.13   Before and After

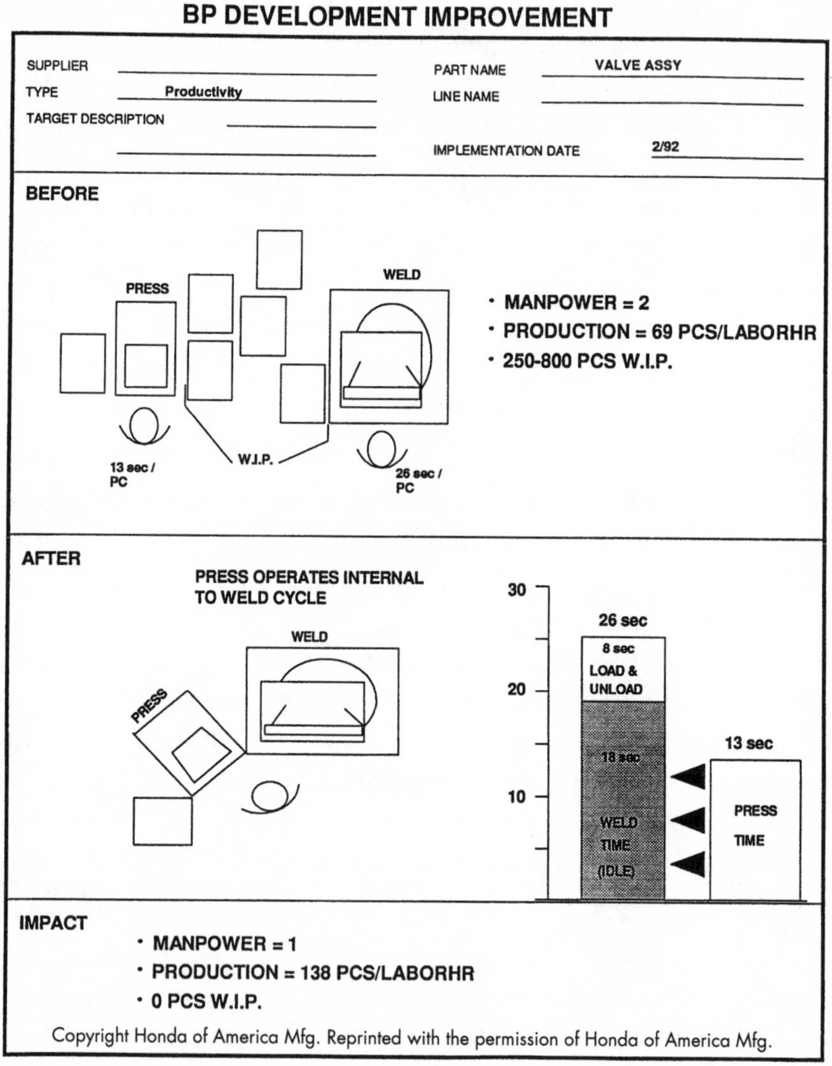

BP DEVELOPMENT IMPROVEMENT

SUPPLIER	_____	PART NAME	**VALVE ASSY**
TYPE	**Productivity**	LINE NAME	_____
TARGET DESCRIPTION	_____		
	_____	IMPLEMENTATION DATE	**2/92**

BEFORE

WELD

PRESS

· **MANPOWER = 2**
· **PRODUCTION = 69 PCS/LABORHR**
· **250-800 PCS W.I.P.**

13 sec /
PC

W.I.P.

26 sec /
PC

AFTER

PRESS OPERATES INTERNAL
TO WELD CYCLE

WELD

PRESS

30 —

26 sec

8 sec
LOAD &
UNLOAD

20 —

13 sec

18 sec

PRESS
TIME

10 —

WELD
TIME
(IDLE)

IMPACT
· **MANPOWER = 1**
· **PRODUCTION = 138 PCS/LABORHR**
· **0 PCS W.I.P.**

Copyright Honda of America Mfg. Reprinted with the permission of Honda of America Mfg.

aisle. After filling the tub, he turned to the workstation and resumed production. By tracing the parts movement from receiving to the line, the BP team discovered:

1. Parts were received 150 pieces per box with 8 boxes per skid.

2. The Shipping Department opened all boxes and put the contents into large metal baskets.

3. The material handler transferred the baskets to the line. The operator walked to retrieve parts from the basket in the aisle, because the basket was too big to fit within reach of the operator.

When a BP team member asked why parts were being repacked into metal containers, he learned that the original reason, that no

Figure 7.14 Delivery Waste

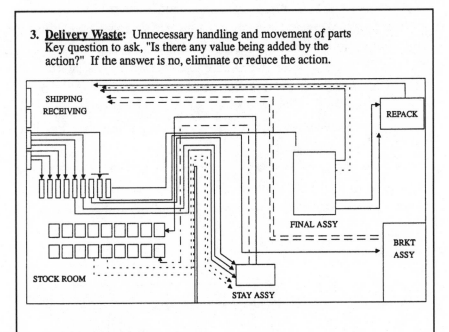

3. **Delivery Waste:** Unnecessary handling and movement of parts Key question to ask, "Is there any value being added by the action?" If the answer is no, eliminate or reduce the action.

Characteristics:
- Component containers too large.
- Component containers cumbersome to open/handle.
- Excess material handling equipment.
- Excess storage racks.
- Complex material handling routing.
- Permanent, expensive material handling devices.
- Lack of integrated processes.
- Poorly designed component delivery layout.
- Poor C.O.P. Travel around items that don't need to be there.
- Forklifts traveling empty.

cardboard was allowed on the shop floor, no longer existed. The BP solution? Parts were brought to the line in their original cardboard boxes and delivered to the operator at their point of use on the line via roller conveyors. The operator no longer had to leave the work cell to retrieve components, and shipping and receiving also did not repack components into large metal containers.

Waste #4, Waste in the Work Itself©

Although most manufacturing pros understand the need for efficient setups, in reality most companies treat mold/die change as break time from production, a time when the crew can take as much time as they need. Changeover becomes a necessary task, with little thought given to lost production. Rather, BP dictates that now is the time when the intensity level should rise, rather than slack off.

There is inherent waste in processes that require setups and changeovers, for example, a mold change at a plastic injection-molding supplier. BP compares this type of waste to an auto racing pit stop. One of the Tasman (racing) CART teams outfitted with Honda engines visited the Marysville Auto Plant and demonstrated

Figure 7.15   Intensity Graph

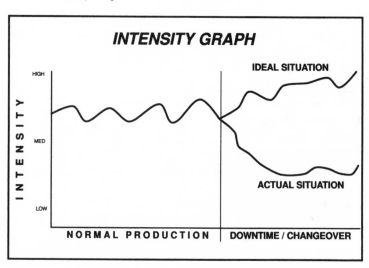

pit stops for associates. A Tasman pit crew tire change team member explained what makes an efficient, winning pit stop:

1. Preparation—All tools are ready, in place, even before the car returns to the pits. Each member of the team knows exactly what must done, and how to do it *the same way each time.*

2. Execution—The key to an efficient pit stop is not the speed at which the workers work, but the smoothness of their actions.

Races are won and lost in the pits, and for every second that your car stays in the pits, the competition is out on the track, passing you by.

Waste #5, Inventory

Inventory is a yardstick of how we do business, and one of the indicators of Waste in the Work Itself is excess inventory. All inventory—raw material, work in process, and finished product—should be at an absolute minimum; by-product wastes of inventory waste include high carrying costs, transit damage, and excess material handling systems.

Waste #6, Wasted Operator Movement

Any movement in which the operator does not add value to the part is waste. Although this form of waste must be reduced or eliminated, it is difficult to detect because this type of waste cannot be casually observed. We tend to confuse motion with work. The BP solution? Ask what value is being added by the movement.

"IT SURE MAKES THE DAY FLY BY!"

A recent BP project conducted with Jefferson Industries of Columbus, Ohio, a stamping supplier, clearly identified big savings from elimination of wasted operator movement. Jefferson's model line had six processes, three of which fed a final welding operation. While practicing the 3 A's, the BP team noticed a final operator, Karen Olsen, moving "at the speed of light," and when the team counted and tallied up her footsteps, the total mileage was a shock —over eight miles per shift! Her shoes told the story. A pair of leather work shoes were worn out from the inside; turning and spinning wore out the heels as well.

The BP solution? The BP team and maintenance created a simple fixture to gravity feed parts closer to the operator, but Karen resisted the change. She tried the new process. It only required two half turns to retrieve parts, and after a week or so, Karen decided "It gives me more time to inspect my welds. I'm less tired when I get home!"

Waste #7, Waste from Rejected Parts

Manufacturing's most important, repeatable task is learning how to produce well and learning exactly what makes a quality part. One of the quickest ways to improve productivity is to eliminate rejected parts because every reject includes not only the loss of that product but also the loss of the opportunity to make a good part. All five other types of waste can and do in fact result in rejects, but when these wastes are identified and eliminated, the search for root cause is an easier process to follow.

All these marvelous tools—the 3A's, the Seven Wastes, the philosophy of BP, worker empowerment—are of no value if, as Mr. Honda said, they are not brought to life by action. Imagine a fisherman walking into the finest sporting goods store in town. He walks out with all the fly-fishing books, all the tackle on the shelves, but he never puts a line in the water. He may know a lot about fly-fishing, but he's never landed a trout!

The BP philosophy and BP tools are the most powerful method a manufacturing operation can use to rapidly unleash the creativity and energy of empowered associates. It's a competitive advantage you cannot help but take. Put your line in the water and see how Honda BP is lived out in the 13-week experience!

8

BP, 13 Weeks to Success

Introduction

I n this chapter, we will put "legs" to the BP philosophy by reviewing the flow of a typical 13-week BP project, using specific steps and examples. The process works well either internally at your own manufacturing facility or externally with your supply base. The only difference between the application of BP to these two areas is the selection process used at the start of the project, either a Model Line Selection process or the Supplier Selection process.

The BP project, like all Honda improvement initiatives, follows Deming's Plan Do Check Act (PDCA) model.

Plan

- ⊛ Supplier Selection (External Focus)
- ⊛ Model Line Selection (Internal Focus)

Step one of the selection process, deciding which supplier or which line on which to begin improvement efforts, is critical because informed selections allow the creation of an environment for success. This is not the time for "shoot from the hip" thinking. The BP team conducts a detailed analysis to ensure a successful start. On most projects, this phase takes one to two weeks' dedicated team time.

Supplier Selection (External) Using the Supplier Selection Matrix

No organization can attack all improvement problems in its supply chain simultaneously. BP pioneers needed a method to set BP

Figure 8.1   Deming's PDCA Circle

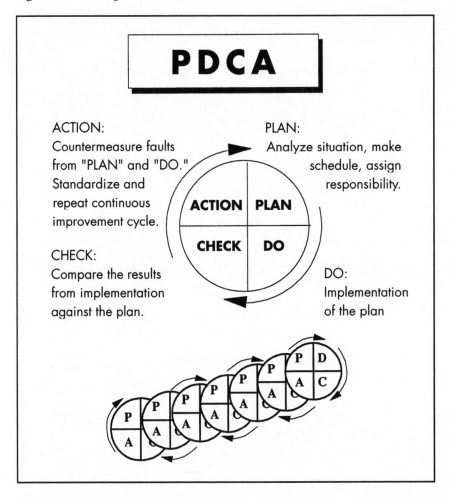

priorities and dedicate specific resources. Although many methods are available, most methods focus on only one aspect of the supplier's need, housekeeping, for example, or work flow. Because Honda procurement needed competitive performance from its supply base, and the quality department needed support for chronic issues, the Supplier Selection Matrix emerged as the most effective prioritizing tool.

The Supplier Selection Matrix is designed to remove, through a series of four steps, any possible subjectivity in the selection process. The first step is to select the precise parameters to which the BP activity will be confined, the entire supply base, for example, or a commodity group within it.

The second step is the determination of selection criteria, or key measurables common to all suppliers to be compared in the matrix. Key measurables typically include the total unit dollars produced by suppliers, the delivery performance or quality level as measured in parts per million rejects, and cost competitiveness as measured by quoted cost against the target cost.

Next, the BP team completes the matrix, filling it in by gathering the appropriate data for each supplier that fits the chosen criteria. Developing a numeric system to rank the options is a great help to making decisions. Next, the BP team analyzes the matrix and selects the best candidates.

The top scorer, however, is not automatically selected because the process of selection is not simply a formula, but an exercise in prioritizing based on facts. Review each of the top scores in consideration of the long-term commodity strategy, the projected program life of the supplied parts, and the past working relationship with the supplier. The addition of these other factors in the matrix will show the priority of supplier selection.

THE SUPPLIER MANAGEMENT MEETING

When the Supplier Selection Matrix is complete, purchasing meets with top management of the selected suppliers to give an overview of the BP project and the amount and type of management commitment required. Management commitment must extend beyond a simple agreement to participate in the BP project. For many suppliers, commitment calls for a complete change of thinking at the supplier's organization.

Finding a Project Manager

Every successful BP project dedicates at least one full-time supplier associate, typically a middle-management associate with very strong people and communication skills, who will exercise strong project management skills throughout the project and beyond. This person becomes the pointman for the supplier.

Companies often pick the wrong project leader for continuous improvement initiatives. The temptation, of course, is to dedicate someone who can be spared, who is politically safe, or "manageable," or who is in a staff position. But picking the wrong leader dooms the project, and so Honda asks that the person chosen to lead supplier BP team members be such a valuable resource in the company that it hurts to dedicate that person to the project. This project team leader must be viewed as a future leader in the supplier organization, and usually that person turns up in production or engineering.

Assigning a key resource to the project has a second objective. It visibly demonstrates management's commitment to improvement.

THE WAR ROOM

BP team members and supporters need a meeting room where they can converge regularly, and where they post data, project findings and ideas, and track results on the walls. The choice of space speaks to the way the project itself works. A visually well-managed, effective room teaches everyone the value of visual management on the floor. Although to many companies the term *War Room* suggests crisis management, to BP associates the War Room has come to signify the core of the War on Waste.

A team member's office, however, will not work as the War

Room. The team leader's old job responsibilities can too easily slip back onto his shoulders. BP activities take on an intensity in time and space that requires a dedicated work area—the War Room—away from the production floor and other distractions. Furnish the room with a conference table and chairs, blackboards or whiteboards, a telephone, and plenty of wall space or large bulletin boards.

Cost Management, Cost Sharing

Cost reduction and cost sharing are key results of all BP projects, and preparation for any BP initiative includes very clear discussions and full and uncompromising agreement up front. Honda's cost-sharing philosophy is to share the "cost down" generated by the project on a 50/50 basis with the supplier, through the unit part cost.

Honda makes no up-front charges to suppliers for their participation in BP because the objective—to generate continuous improvement—is the real payoff. The merit, or payoff, is the merit that is shared; savings are agreed up front to be shared 50/50. Overall, true long-term merit for the customer/supplier team is the creation of a strong, self-reliant organization that will continue to grow. Honda sees no better embodiment of the partnering spirit than this approach to productivity benefits.

BP Project Scheduling

Having reached agreement on cost reduction, cost sharing, the War Room, and dedicated project leadership, the team sets a project start date. Suppliers can expect to see Honda BP associates on site 3 or 4 days per week for 13 weeks.

It is important for team leaders to be sensitive to the start and finish of weekly production at the supplier facility; typical BP days, therefore, run Tuesday through Thursday. Further, Honda BP pros typically keep several BP sites in process simultaneously with follow-up visits; keeping a clear schedule for the length of the project is crucial.

Do

Step 1, BP training

Honda conducts a six- to eight-hour training class, "Honda BP Training," for all prospective team members to familiarize them with tools and techniques that will be used throughout the project. Topics covered in detail include:

Figure 8.2   Orientation

> **Basic Philosophies:**
>   A. Associate involvement
>   B. Minimum investment—Intro to Phase II
>   C. Raw material utilization (yield)
>   D. Spec BP
>   E. Identify and eliminate waste (7 wastes)
>   F. COPDS (wall, closet, kitchen, visibility strategies)
>   G. 3A's
>   H. Deming Circle (PDCA)
>   I. 8 categories—25 items
>   J. Displaced associates
> **Basic tools:**
>   A. Calculations
>   B. Forms

Attendees typically use the BP Manual as the core text. The class usually includes three to five suppliers. Class can be conducted at the supplier site or at Honda.

Step 2, Situation Analysis I (SAI)

In this two- to three-day phase, Honda team members develop a thorough understanding of the supplier and the parts they supply. Associates conduct this project phase at the Honda plant, lineside,

Figure 8.3   Situation Analysis #1

Situation Analysis #1

Definition: To separate something into its parts in order to study it or better understand it.

Situation Analysis #1 is the gathering of all information available at Honda about a supplier and the parts they supply. This analysis is performed by the Honda BP team before their first visit to the supplier and is repeated at each facility that receives parts from the supplier.

Areas Analyzed:

1. **Lineside at Manufacturing Facility.**
   - View parts being assembled to automobile.
   - Understand Fit/Function to car.
   - Discuss parts with associates and team leaders to find out any problems, concerns, requests for changes, etc.

2. **Material Service.**
   - Discuss delivery situation with associates.
   - Further review packaging situation.

3. **Auto Parts Quality (APQ).**
   Meet with supplier associates to discuss quality situation.
   - PPM levels – current & trend.
   - Potential part changes.
   - Current/past problems.
   - Response to quality problems.

4. **Parts Procurement Group (PPG).**
   Meet with supplier associates to understand delivery situation.
   - Delivery PPM levels - current & trend.
   - Logistics of parts (where & how they are delivered). If MEI, Visit.
   - Current/past problems.
   - Applications of supplier parts.
   - Response to delivery problems/requests (flexibility).

5. **Procurement.**
   Meet with supplier associates to understand procurement situations.
   - Review & understand quotes.
   - What type of pricing is used? Target or formula?
   - What has been the supplier competitive history?
   - What is procurement's short/long-term strategy for the supplier and/or individual parts.

6. **Quality Engineering Department (QED).**
   Meet with supplier associates to understand engineering situation.
   - Understand warranty situation of suppliers parts.
   - Understand open/potential design change/manufacturing instructions involving supplier parts.

following the 3 A's philosophy of going to the actual spot to see the actual parts. BP team members talk to the production area team leader and plant associates who assemble the parts on the vehicle. The task is to gain firsthand knowledge of how that part flows through the Honda assembly process—what the part looks like in the vehicle, its function, any mating part issues, and packaging logistics. Team members study the part's quality and delivery history by meeting with Parts Quality and Production Procurement associates. The Cost Procurement department contributes to part unit cost history.

The Situation Analysis step has proven to be well worth the time investment with all projects. Honda associates study supplier companies and learn more from the process than the immediate parts data. Many participating companies have expressed pleasure at learning the Honda team's knowledge of their company and components; suppliers feel confident at the beginning of the process that if team members put the same amount of effort into the project that they put into understanding their company and its parts, the BP project is a guaranteed success.

Step 3, supplier orientation meeting

"Begin with the end in mind."
Steven Covey,
Seven Habits of Highly Effective People

BP Orientation marks the first full day of the project at the supplier's facility. These meetings are important because they heighten plant-wide awareness of the BP project—its philosophy, basic methodology, and goals. BP team members meet and quickly set up the War Room, where they informally meet management staff and prepare to communicate the goals of the project to the workforce.

A "town meeting," a 30-minute, preshift informal gathering of all employees, works well to communicate project goals and plans. The town meeting approach fulfills two distinct needs—the meeting communicates to the entire workforce management's total commitment to improvement, and it informally introduces Honda staffers. The town meeting encourages employees to ask specific questions about the project as it sets the tone for breaking down any barriers that exist in their minds. Bringing all associates and team members together in the same place at the same time also dispels hidden agendas about change. And best of all, the meeting gives the project a powerful jump start.

Honda team members prepare for the meeting so that they can answer most expected questions. Most frequently associates ask, "How will this affect me in my job?" or "Are you going to evaluate me?" Sometimes associates say "Start on my line. It's the most screwed up!"

At this point, the team is a team in name only; the BP project is an "arranged marriage" in which each partner is wondering what to do first. However, this is a natural process for the Honda BP members. Although early discussions by the team will help determine how and when the team will update management on progress, the most important agenda item for the supplier orientation meeting is to set the final presentation date. Setting the final presentation date on the first day of the initiative signals to the team that the project is now running, and the end date will drive every element of the project, every team member's activities. The priority is clear.

Step 4, model line selection

> *"Let the data lead you."*
>
> Dorian Shainin,
> Shewhart Award Winner

The area targeted for BP work may be a production line, a specific process, or an entire department. Whatever the target, however, it must match the scope and timing of the project. BP is a long-term process of activities delivered through 13-week projects, and so it is especially important to be sure that each area or "model line" targeted for improvement meets the time parameters to guarantee completion of the goal on time to the presentation date.

The mechanism BP uses to decide which area to focus on is the Model Line Selection Matrix. The matrix organizes the existing empirical data for all lines in the plant by defining the key measurables related to productivity, including:

- The average daily production versus the requirement;

- Pieces per labor hour;

- Reject rate for the line;

- Line balance percentage (the percentage of value-added time in a multiprocess line); and

- Manpower.

At the beginning of many BP projects, the supplier may have already selected the line on which they want to focus. At Parker Hannifin's Jonesboro, Arkansas, plant, management picked Line C, the air-conditioning pipeline. Although the BP team did not argue management's "decision," they wanted to develop a Model Line Selection Matrix anyway to teach the team the technique. The matrix showed that Jonesboro's biggest opportunity existed on air-conditioning pipeline B.

The production manager acknowledged that their recommendation, determined purely through intuition, was the wrong choice. Project results—hard data—reinforced the selection of pipeline B.

Breakthroughs in One Hour!

After model line selection, the BP team meets for approximately one hour with model line associates. This meeting is marked by much more open communication; the stage is now set for future activity. Typical employee responses are pride in being chosen for the BP activity, or frustration that they are to be singled out for attention. Because so much of the lasting success rests on these associates, the meeting must be structured to allow all these feelings and attitudes to surface and be answered.

One approach to building trust with model line associates is to ask for their suggestions. The goal is participation, including associate's ideas, and the best way to make that happen is to build trust. Expect the response to be silence. But, when team members ask if the associates have any complaints, one or two will be voiced. These complaints are like rejects uncovered and analyzed in the production process. They are valuable gifts that will move the group from helpless complaints to actively thinking about solutions— "What suggestion can you make to correct this concern?" Often what truly generates associates' interest in the activity is team willingness to hear their concerns linked with a suggestion or proposed solution.

In just 45 minutes, by meeting with line associates, BP has accomplished a major breakthrough in their understanding and support of the project.

Step 5, baseline data collection

Many continuous improvement activities start with a shot and a cloud of dust, followed by chaos that takes weeks or months to undo. Some quick-hit improvement programs skip this essential step, and suppliers and their customers pay the price. The urgency for results shortcuts the process of understanding the entire situation. The solution is to collect baseline data and create a snapshot of how the model line is performing at the start of the project.

BP calls collecting key measurables "before" data, and the measurables are similar to those collected for the Model Line Selection Matrix. Baseline data, however, may include other key measurables that are particular to the model line processes, the number of component part variations, machine cycle times, and associate cycle times.

There are two rules to remember in data collection:

1. Performance data must include previous two to three months' history. Three months, or a series, are always better than two.

2. Be clear on how data is calculated now and in the two to three months' history, because 13 weeks later, the data must be calculated exactly the same way to accurately measure project results.

Two engineers assigned to the Parker Hannifin Batesville, Mississippi, project were anxious to get started and make some big changes. Project members restrained them, however, when they told the pair that the first thing they had to do was to gather baseline data. They felt apprehensive—"This exercise would be a complete waste of good engineers' time!"

At the end of the first week, all data was assembled in various reports. Things started to look different, and the engineers realized that they were beginning to develop a new understanding of their company. They had never had so much contact with so many different departments! They became experts in company reporting after having dug into dozens of company reports, all invaluable sources of numbers that told their story. Finally, one engineer admitted to having new confidence based on certain and complete understanding of the model line performance. By moving these professionals into a different role in their company, BP removed an unhealthy acceptance of the status quo, and transformed them into improvement pioneers.

Figure 8.4   Key Measurables

1. Model Line Downtime (%) =

$$\frac{\text{(Scheduled Run Hours - Actual Run Hours)}}{\text{Scheduled Run Hours}} \quad \text{X 100}$$

2. Production Per Manhour $= \dfrac{\text{Total Good Pieces Produced}}{\text{Total Direct Labor Hours Used}}$

3. Scrap Percentage $= \dfrac{\text{Total Pieces Scrapped}}{\text{Total Pieces Produced}} \quad \text{X 100}$

4. Daily Production = total good pieces produced in one day
   (can be either 1, 2, or 3 shifts).

5. Manpower - How many direct labor people are working on the line.

6. Line Balance

$$\frac{\text{Sum of each Individual Process}}{\text{(longest process x \# of processes)}} \quad \text{or} \quad \frac{\text{Sum of each Individual Process}}{\text{(machine cycle x \# of processes)}}$$

7. Production Efficiency

$$\frac{\text{Process Standard Time X Number of Parts Produced (in hundreds)}}{\text{Direct Hours Charged}}$$

8. Material Yield (%)

$$\frac{\text{Pieces Produced X Raw Material Weight of Finished Part}}{\text{Raw Material Used}} \quad \text{X 100}$$

9. Throughput Time - How long does it take 1 part to get through
   the Model Line process.

10. Square Foot of Floor Space - How many square feet of floor
    space is currently being dedicated to the Model Line. This
    may be broken down into factory space and warehouse space.

11. Inventory Levels - What is the average dollar value of
    the finished goods, WIP & component parts associated
    with the Model Line.

12. Rework Percentage $= \dfrac{\text{Number of Parts Reworked}}{\text{Total Parts Produced}} \quad \text{X 100}$

13. Direct Ship % $= \dfrac{\text{Total Parts Produced - (\#Rework + \#Scrapped)}}{\text{Total Parts Produced}} \quad \text{X 100}$

14. 35mm Slides - Take numerous shots to illustrate current
    conditions on the line. Concentrate on:

    - COP areas   - Layout
    - Safety concerns

15. Video of the Model Line - Also used to illustrate current
    conditions but is frequently used for time studies and
    in-depth analysis.

16. Material Travel Distance - Measure/calculate the actual distance
    that each component/part travels in feet during the Model Line
    Process. This can be presented as one distance, which is the
    sum of each component/part.

Step 6, Situation Analysis II (SAII)

Situation Analysis II takes the biggest percentage of project time. In this phase, BP members thoroughly investigate the model line, following the precepts of the 3A's. The team begins to develop a detailed understanding of model line processes by working closely with the model line associates.

The team collects mounds of data for analysis. The data is then formulated into tools for improvement. COPDS and the use of strategies are used by the team when they begin to physically clean the line. BPrs identify the Seven Wastes, and they document their findings through charts, graphs, and sketches. Videotaping the line and taking 35mm slides document the existing line and process conditions prior to any improvement implementation.

Management is usually shocked by the intensity of this exercise. In fact, Dave Smith, a production supervisor, thought he knew it all. After 20 years in production, he was sure where the opportunities lay hidden. But when he studied the line and looked at the actual parts, he had an epiphany—"After five years being out there on that floor, nothing helped me see the situation as well as the BP Situation Analysis!"

SITUATION ANALYSIS II TOOLS

The Lost Time Graph is a very powerful tool and a revelation for many companies. The Lost Time Graph shows the amount of time required to meet an average daily production requirement, compared to an extrapolated time to meet production, based on a time study; the difference between the two is called lost time. Lost time can be broken down into as many segments as can be identified. The graph's unique approach, therefore, is that it highlights what is missing, rather than "what is here." These segments could include setup time, downtime, early/late breaks, late start-ups, and component shortages.

In 1997, Parker Hannifin's Batesville air-conditioning hose plant manager was caught off guard by the Lost Time Graph. He had never seen the cumulative effect of various lost items on production displayed in such a revealing format. He stormed out of the BP Room, furious. Several minutes later he returned, blood pressure back in place, eager to remedy the waste highlighted by the Lost Time Graph.

Pareto charts of downtime and rejects are another powerful tool. Associates on the line are as frustrated as everyone else when rejects and downtime plague their productivity performance. Unfortunately, BP teams frequently encounter these marvelous tools misapplied with few measurable, lasting results. We know that by determining the root cause of defects and the countermeasure of these defects, using pareto analysis, BP projects will move well in Situation Analysis II.

QUICK SUCCESSES

During this phase, associates may occasionally give team members an improvement idea, and it is absolutely essential, as in the Reynosa story in Chapter 1, that BP team members be prepared to implement a good idea immediately. "Quick success" items gain associate trust, and release energy for the long haul.

Step 7, goal setting

Situation Analysis II leads to project goals; the goals must be SMART—**S**pecific, **M**easurable, **A**chievable, **R**ealistic, and **T**imely. Goals cannot be subjective. They are calculated from the "before" data and situation analysis results. Finally, goal-setting specific to each project sets the priority for the remainder of the project.

Step 8, develop improvement ideas

Toward the end of the situation analysis, the team will individually begin to formulate some ideas for improvement. These ideas frequently come from brainstorming sessions, so if the basic rules of brainstorming are observed, the exercise will be very beneficial to all members of the team.

Tom Kiely, BP Marysville veteran, believes that "Iron sharpens iron," and one idea is enhanced by another. Keeping the team goals in focus during the idea development process is one of the most energetic and enthusiastic times for the project. As the team works at developing ideas, model line associate ideas must also be harvested. If the team has implemented a few quick success items, the gathering of these new ideas from associates should be easy.

BP uses an Idea Tracking Chart to control ideas and to formally track and record their implementation.

By enlarging the chart and posting it at the model line, associates can view the progress of their ideas through to implementation. Post *all* ideas on the tracking chart, although some ideas will never

Figure 8.5 Rules of Brainstorming

Rules of Brainstorming

- Never criticize ideas.

- Write down each idea.

- Agree on the question or issue being brainstormed, and write it down.

- Record the speaker's words on a flip chart without interpretation.

- Complete the brainstorming session in 5 to 15 minutes.

make it to implementation due to conflicts with other ones or incompatibility with project goals.

The team must then meet with the idea's creator to fully understand the idea and benefit, or tell the associate why the idea is not scheduled for implementation. Sometimes the idea will be changed to meet project goals, however, but never without input from the associate, because ideas have an ownership quality to which the team must always be sensitive.

Step 9, implementation plan

During this phase, engineering and maintenance are brought on board. They must be aware of the dedication of time and resources that they are expected to provide to implement associates' ideas. BP uses a detailed milestone chart showing all the implementation items. The list is in priority order so that the timing of implementation is tied to responsible parties with appropriate completion dates.

Step 10, implementation, the longest day

After the schedule is developed, team responsibilities take on many forms, such as implementation or expediting, as they continue in their analysis role. The team has the responsibility to implement as many ideas on the schedule as they can with their limited resources, a balance that helps lighten the load for maintenance and engineering. As expediters, the team must ensure that all other departments' implementation items are completed as detailed by the schedule. They must identify critical items and those that may be dropping behind, and they must expedite the laggards so that they do not affect the overall schedule.

Frequently during implementation, the BP team reaches a stopping point where they must wait for a department to complete their tasks. When this happens, the team should return to the analysis phase of the model line, or choose another area in which to start the BP process.

Figure 8.6 Project Management

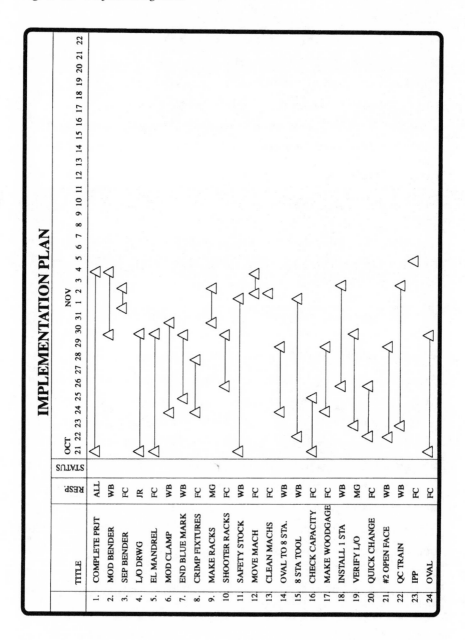

Implementation is the most intense time for the project, but if the team has developed a detailed and expedited plan, implementation should roll with no major obstacles.

Midcourse Corrections

BP experts recommend establishing an inventory buffer to cover downtime caused by implementation. Further, allow for proper adjustments to any revision to the processes or area layout, and try to accurately estimate downtime for actual implementation to guarantee adequate coverage.

Additional inventory to cover the adjustment period is key to project success and to the morale of model line associates. Following complete implementation and resumption of production, the model line will shut down whenever required to countermeasure problems and make further improvements, but this adjustment will not be possible when associates are under pressure to produce parts for a shipment. PDCA is practiced during this phase.

Preparing for Line Associates' Reactions

Be prepared for deep apprehension from line associates on the first day after changes are implemented. Even with all the meetings and communication conducted lineside to explain ideas and changes, the associates will have very little confidence that the new layout will work. Some associates may remark that "whether it worked or not, we were stuck with it."

Line associates will be shocked to find the entire BP team lined up for early Monday morning start-up. The team is there to help answer new equipment or process questions, to help catch up when the line falls behind, and to add moral support. Associates always react very positively to this new approach toward support, and by

Figure 8.7   12-Month Basic Schedule

12-MONTH BASIC SCHEDULE

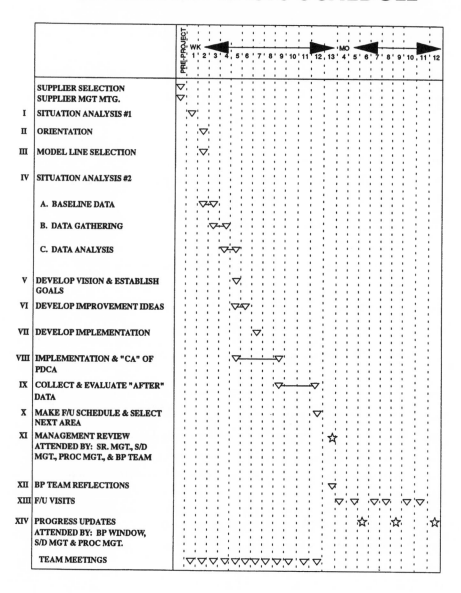

lunchtime they feel more confident about the new line, and they show it with eager offers to assist further improvements. It is the longest day of the project; frequently teams split up to follow the same support detail for other shifts. This iterative process continues until all associates on the model line are comfortable with the changes.

CHECK

Step 1, collect and evaluate "after" data

After the line has stabilized for about one week, the team begins to gather data to compare to the baseline, or the "before" snapshot. Make this tracking period as long as possible, but time constraints of the project usually do not allow more than two to three weeks. Calculate the "after" data for each of the goals the same way the "before" data was computed. Apples to oranges comparisons won't work.

Collect "after" data on the goal items in a matrix that shows how well the team performed against the goals. If the goals were not reached, the matrix should show what countermeasures can be implemented to reach the goal.

Step 2, develop long-term organizational plan

The BP project is the method of introducing a continuous improvement process. It systematically teaches the techniques and tools to make that improvement a part of the supplier's organization, and so the improvement philosophy must, to become reality, follow the supplier's strategic direction. The BP team does not do this type of planning; senior supplier management conducts it, and the results of their work should be presented during the Celebration of Results.

Step 3, Celebration of Results

Honda BP associates learned a lesson from one supplier engineer who had for two years conducted BP projects in his organization. The regular project format concludes projects with an evaluation meeting when Honda and supplier management personnel sit together up front to view the results presentation. Usually both management teams ask questions or make comments at the end, addressing any strengths or weaknesses.

But, unfortunately for the supplier, one of their post-Honda evaluations concluded with criticism of many aspects of the project. Gary Griffin, a very wise and thoughtful engineer, decided then and there to change the name of the presentation from "Project Evaluation Meeting" to "Celebration of Results."

The Celebration of Results is designed to be a springboard to future activities. This gathering is not the time to evaluate and critique the BP activity, but to celebrate the marvelous results achieved when the team put a little focus on an opportunity area.

Make the Celebration of Results as positive and upbeat as possible. Gary Griffin issued invitations, rather than meeting notices, and filled the BP Room with balloons and team photos, colorful decorations, and a few charts taken from the actual project. He laid a banquet table with juices and snacks. The room was transformed. A three-foot square cake in the shape of the plant made it a real party.

Overkill you might say? But to which kind of event would you like to be invited—an evaluation or a celebration?

This chapter has covered a few very simple and very powerful tools that BP practitioners use for every project, from gathering and using data to unleashing the power of associates through their suggestions and their participation in the BP project itself. Each step begins with hard data, and each one takes participating associates a little closer to excellence, and a little more in control of their own destinies.

Figure 8.8   Track Actual Performance Against the Goal

ACTUAL VS. GOAL

PROCESS	CYCLE TIMES:		CAUSE	COUNTERMEASURE
	GOAL	ACTUAL		
BEND 1	13.4	16.3	1. BENDER OPERATING TOO SLOWLY. 2. PIPES ON WRONG SIDE OF OPERATOR. 3. CAPS & O-RINGS NOT EASY TO REACH	1. SPEED UP BENDER 2. SUPPLY PARTS TO OPER. RH 3. MAKE NEW BIN TO DISPENSE PARTS NEAR OPER.
CRIMP 1	13.4	13.7	1. LABEL DISPENSER DOES NOT OPERATE PROPERLY. 2. HOSE FIXTURE IS NOT ALIGNED CORRECTLY.	1. REPAIR/REPLACE 2. ALIGN HOSE FIXTURE
BEND 2	13.4	13.9	1. CAPS & O-RINGS NOT EASY TO REACH 2. PIPES FALL OFF OF SHOOTER RACK.	1. MAKE NEW BIN TO DISPENSE PARTS NEAR OPER. 2. ADJUST RACK
CRIMP 2	14.0	15.4	1. PARTS STICK IN FIXTURE. 2. OPERATOR HAS TO TURN TOO FAR TO PICK UP HOSE ASSY.	1. RELIEVE FIXTURE 2. MODIFY RACK TO BRING PARTS NEAR OPERATOR
CLAMP & PACK	10.0	11.1	1. SKID + EMPTY BOX MTL. HANDLING NOT CONSISTENT. 2. OPERATOR HAS TO WALK TOO FAR.	1. MARK LOCATIONS FOR SKIDS AND BOXES 2. EXTEND RACK

9

Enterprise Leadership— Take the High Road

INTRODUCTION

G M plant shuts down for the fourth week! Lopez dictates cost cuts! UAW wage and security issues cloud labor talks. Fear of outsourcing paralyzes purchasers. Headlines like these point to continued confusion and loss of direction among major auto producers and their suppliers. Leadership during periods of disintegration and reformation of mature industries takes vision and consistency throughout an organization. Leadership for the lean enterprise requiries a focus on excellence in people, systems, and the extended enterprise that is only found among industry leaders who practice what they teach. Contrast the Lopez tactic of launching his "warriors," to Honda's and Chrysler's dispatch supplier development experts.

But enticing a giant and all its enterprise partners to completely reform its supply base practice takes more than vision. For the suppliers, simple, powerful, practical methods are what small- and medium-sized suppliers need. Visible leadership, like that offered by Chrysler's former head of purchasing Thomas Stallkamp, must be supported by day-to-day purchasing procedures that ring true to management's stated objectives. Chrysler's development program, SCORE, for example, has met with great success among suppliers. Other programs and purchasing personalities, like Lopez's, have had far less successful results. PICOS, GM's supplier development program, for example, has been criticized for being more of a "hit and run" tactic, leaving suppliers with no better process maturity after the departure of GM consultants.

LEADERSHIP MEANS VISION

As companies and industries move through their life cycles, they require different leadership styles from different types of leaders to carry them forward. Lee Iacocca was the perfect leader for his time at Chrysler. Only a "car guy" and a supreme marketer could take the struggling giant, weighed down with exponential product and parts proliferation, and convince both the U. S. government and the consumer of his comeback plans. Iacocca told the public what he planned to do to save Chrysler, and his tactics reflected his turnaround strategy.

Honda is not the only producer doing something right with suppliers. Chrysler's Stallkamp, like Iacocca, has almost single-handedly turned around Chrysler's reputation with suppliers by developing programs to support and reach suppliers and gain their confidence. Almost every week we hear about Chrysler's purposeful development of its extended enterprise supply network. At one point in his career, Stallcamp was head of Chrysler's in-house parts business, a position that no doubt gave him a unique perspective on the blunt end of how suppliers felt, how their flexibility and responsiveness are tested daily. Stallkamp learned how *not* to do it.

Stallkamp's suppliers have learned that they can trust their customer, and Chrysler is beginning to reap the benefits of having worked at improving their relationships. Further, with the highest profit per car of any automaker in North America, Chrysler is a great example of industry leadership. Chrysler, and others who strive to take a leadership position, carry a bigger, global vision as they grow and transform.

Soichiro Honda's vision always extended to becoming a global producer of vehicles that would be bigger and faster than small motorbikes. Honda learned early on the absolute necessity of supplier/partner support when his motorcycle suppliers carried him into the "closed" auto business.

Other less well-known examples of small companies with big visions abound. Winston Chen and Ko Nishimura, founders of billion-dollar electronics giant Solectron, always ran the company, even when it occupied a much fought-over position in the second-tier board production market, as a first-tier global producer. They built their customer base and their engineering and sales philosophy to support and grow that vision.

Leadership for the Lean Enterprise

Industry leadership for the extended enterprise goes far beyond mechanically plugging in customers and suppliers in a superficial attempt at partnership. Procurement and manufacturing managers want a philosophy-driven approach that will take them, along with their supply base, into a competitive position described as lean, or agile. The customer/supplier connections must be facilitated by excellent communications systems, the absolute best professionals available installed at both ends of the relationship, and management support and encouragement to partners under an umbrella philosophy that looks at the greater good for the entire enterprise.

The lean, or agile enterprise, works as a single entity, and performs at a competitive speed that allows producers to respond quickly, at lower cost, to customer requirements or market shifts. In the information transfer industry, Federal Express and Netscape are lean and agile; the U.S. Postal Service, unfortunately, is not. In the information storage industry, EMC Corporation, a Massachusetts high-tech miracle, is lean and flexible, while your public library most probably is not. In the clothing business, Levi with its custom-cut and deliver-to-order jeans is agile and flexible, as is J.S. Bank; Brooks Brothers is not. Knock-down, assemble-it-yourself furniture outlets are lean; Baker and Henredon are not.

Obviously, some of these producers are not striving for quickness. They believe, in the case of very high-quality furniture makers, that their customers above all want unique quality, and that they are willing to wait for it. Clearly, that approach is unacceptable throughout the auto industry. With the exception of custom-built vehicles, such as Porsche specials, Honda NSX, and Rolls Royce, the entire industry must move to lean manufacturing. Jim Womack, author of *Lean Thinking*[5] and co-author of the groundbreaking *The Machine that Changed the World*, believes that lean thinking must follow these five principles:

1. Precisely specify *value* by specific product.
2. Identify the *value stream* for each product.
3. Make value *flow* without interruptions.
4. Let the customer *pull* value from the producer.
5. Pursue *perfection*.

Womack's five principles all apply to the automotive extended enterprise, whose competitive objective has transformed industry focus from pushing products to providing value for the customer. Value means a combination of perfect quality and competitive pricing, with life-of-the-vehicle quality service support. Value does not necessarily mean the lowest sticker on the window. For many consumers, the cost of a new car represents nearly one year's salary, or more, and the financial and human cost-to-own plus the final residual or trade-in value of a vehicle count in a smart consumer's decision.

Suppliers, therefore, represent the "80-percent determinants" of quality and value—generally 80 percent of the cost of the car comes from purchased parts. If suppliers can build in the kind of lifetime quality and cost levels that assemblers and customers love, they will drive the entire industry forward to Womack's vision of a lean enterprise.

Most small- and medium-sized auto suppliers, however, cannot meet these high challenges completely on their own, not simply because the dedication of resources to partnering issues draws on the same essential resources needed to make production, but because, as suppliers, they only represent half of the partnering equation. Communications flows through electronic systems, whether they follow traditional MRP systems, for example, or more sophisticated enterprise resource scheduling, only, like all circuits, work in a closed loop environment. The circuit must be complete for the signal to pass.

Interruptions on the circuit—awkward systems, unclear pull signals, irregular product flow, and noninvolved employees—don't work in a lean enterprise. Womack's five principles address these issues, and specific to supplier development of leanness are the third principle—make value flow without interruption; the fourth principle—let the customer pull value from the producer; and the fifth principle—pursue perfection. For an automotive supplier at the second, third, or even fourth tier, these challenges increase in degree of difficulty as varying customer requirements test their quality and delivery response capabilities.

THE LEAN SUPPLIER

Lean suppliers to Honda, Chrysler, Ford, Nissan, and Toyota are challenged, as the WEK and Toyota brake supplier fire stories demonstrated, to meet uninterrupted product flow requirements. Line-down costs at all producers, even second-tier suppliers to first-tier assemblers, are measured in tens of thousands of dollars per minute. Likewise, quality rejects, just like nondeliveries—parts shipped in too early or too late—cost the same amount in down-time, although auto manufacturers such as Honda have a small amount of buffer protection in their parts consolidation center located one step before the assembly line.

Williams Technologies of Summerville, South Carolina, for example, understands the systems, product flow, and people require-ments to ship very special assemblies to first-tier producers such as Honda, Nissan, Ford, and GM. Williams's workforce and its "Leapfrog" system are designed and empowered to create innovation. For example, most second-tier suppliers of complex assemblies must deal with many variations in components as they build for different customers in different countries. Williams is no stranger to that challenge, one that would prevent most ordinary humans from maintaining in their head a Bill of Material for each possible variation. Not only must workers, even new ones, remember which valves go in which GM assembly, but they must also be familiar enough with the complete assembly process for that assembly to move the component along to its proper next stage. Literacy issues, especially with multilingual workers, can make the difference between product variation built with perfect quality and slower response times with lower quality. If an assembler is most comfort-able reading a Bill of Material or Process Bill in Spanish, English-speaking producers must understand and anticipate the challenge. With several hundred variations and several thousand components, it's a lot to remember.

Williams has devised a unique visible management approach that guarantees that, if a worker can watch TV, he or she can cor-rectly assemble the part. Leapfrog is plant-wide and the system setup puts one terminal and monitor at each workstation, at a cost of about $1,200 per unit; programming is performed by workers themselves. As a new item is ordered, the associate enters compo-nent lists and process information. Williams Technologies President Jeff Anderson believes that this is the right way to empower associates with just the right amount of systems power—a do-it-yourself approach.

Williams's system also provides demanding customers (most of whom are located at least one to two days' transit time away) like GM and Ford a degree of responsiveness and the ability to move from one product to another quickly—another of Womack's requirements for a lean system.

Other lean supplier leaders, like Parker Hannifin's Larry Hopcraft and Progressive's Ruston Simon, understand the challenge to the lean enterprise. Their dedication to workforce development, as indicated by stepping into the BP program without urging, underscores their commitment.

WHAT IS LEADERSHIP FOR THE LEAN ENTERPRISE?

Honda supplier development philosophies are built on the idea that teaching suppliers how to perfect their process and how to become self-reliant, rather than hammering cost savings, will yield long-term, permanent results. The BP goal reflects this extended vision—select a single model line, for example, and work three months on it, with three Honda engineers and three supplier engineers. When that model line works well, the supplier is asked to promulgate the approach through the rest of his shop, and then on to his supply base.

Where is the leadership challenge in this approach? Remember, at the second and third tiers, Honda suppliers inevitably supply competitors like Ford and Chrysler with much more product than the supplier ships to HAM. What suppliers learn from BP raises the bar for everyone. And Honda BP projects are occasionally conducted *directly* on a competitor's line, as the BP team did for Chrysler at the Reynosa, Mexico, TRW plant.

Raising the bar, running a faster and leaner race, requires every member of the extended enterprise to be more and more innovative. BP meets the challenge to be lean by taking waste out of operations. BPII, which perfects capital equipment decisions and plant layouts, answers long-term facility challenges.

BP in Other Industries

BP is also used to raise the level of competitiveness in nonautomotive industries. After seeing BP in action, Parker's Larry Hopcraft, wanting to accentuate his *Targets* internal quality program, asked Honda to allow his company to pair his engineers with Marysville personnel in order to train them faster. "We don't want to wait to learn it," Hopcraft said.

Honda Purchasing's response was that this idea would be relatively impossible, because Honda engineers would be going out specifically to help a number of Parker's competitors, which would, Hopcraft understood, destroy confidentiality. So Hopcraft rephrased his request. "Would Honda give us the BP team for one more 13-week cycle, at our expense, with our jet?" He proposed taking the BP experts out to three different Parker plants, one making propane cylinders, one aircraft parts, and one other non-auto components factory, each located in different corners of the United States. Marysville agreed to this innovative solution.

Taking the High Road

Honda calls this taking the high road. Taking the high road means risking the possibility that Detroit competitors will seize the power of BP for their own competitive advantage. So far none of Detroit's Big Three can point to overall success in the supplier development area. Insiders say one of the missing pieces is lack of management support, where one industry analyst says, "Initiatives like BP separate the men from the boys."

8 to 1 Payback

American companies are criticized for being too bottom-line oriented, too short-sighted to be courageous or visionary where it counts in the area of best practice. They continue to avoid programs that require an investment in manpower, even though, as Honda has learned, the payback is 8 to 1—for each manpower dollar spent, 8 dollars come back in productivity improvement.

Sometimes taking the high road means taking a leadership role and working behind the scenes to leverage excellence. GE had asked for help developing a program that would take one segment of purchasing to world-class levels. The challenge was to discover how to optimize resources in a decentralized organization, something with which many North American giants are struggling. Picking the right leader is the answer. Decentralized organizations often fail at purchasing innovation because someone at the corporate level undermines their attempts at innovation by imposing his own approach on the plants.

The appropriate leadership response is to create a *Tiger Team*, as TRW did, made up of the strongest purchasing managers from the largest divisions, the execs with the most power in the entire company, and put them in charge of worldwide commodity teams in each of the plants. Build their time into the budget, and for 50 percent of that time commitment, make them the decision-makers for the larger corporate entity. TRW took this powerful approach several years ago, as has GE and many other giants that recognize the power of good leadership, taking the high road.

What Doesn't Work—
Leveraging and Bad Metrics

Leadership for the extended enterprise takes more than wielding a blitzkrieg hammer to drive suppliers into submission. As GM has discovered, leveraging, certifying, or auditing suppliers into compliance doesn't produce the desired results either. Other "continuous improvement" methods, largely mechanistic, nonphilosophy-driven approaches produce predictably limited results. And outside consulting is expensive and tends to be impermanent because the consultants spend their time in the executive office, rather than on the shop floor, working with the experts.

Pick the Right Person

If the leader you have chosen to head your improvement initiative is not passionate and driven to make a long-term difference, you have picked the wrong person. If Honda's mission were cost-down only, the results would be seen in a week—"presto, chango." But the mission and, therefore, the methods are different.

Pick the Right Program

Doug Chamberlain, assistant manager of Honda Marysville supplier development group, the headquarters for all North American BP activities, has seen them all. Chamberlain talks regularly with suppliers who have experienced PICOS, GM's improvement program, and similar supplier development initiatives. Chamberlain has attended, and sent several of his people, to other kaizen-type programs. Although some of these for-profit events are tremendously successful, he is concerned that, at best, many of these programs yield only short-term results. "You can show that you had a tremendous impact, but if you revisit that same area a month or so later, you will not see the same results. In fact, one supplier confided that two weeks after a recent PICOS activity, production employees had either changed their area back to its previous condition, or they changed it to something else." This automotive supplier has plants located all over the United States; the plants have performed many PICOS projects and BP activities as well.

In fact, Chamberlain himself, after attending a three-day supplier event, stood up and apologized to his group; he felt that management had abused them by jerking them around, not allowing them to participate as partners. "We [management] just told them [the associates] (during the event) to move machinery around. They weren't asked for their input. It was a rushed atmosphere. It was a one-sided activity, directed down at employees, 'you are going to change this, you will change that,' and the natural, inevitable result was that associates with no ownership rebelled. They made it fail."

Don't Just Do It!

One cause of failure among these processes, Chamberlain believes, is that participants and consultants forget the Deming Circle. Failing, after all the presentations and numbers counting productivity gains and inventory savings, to revisit the floor one or two months later, is a mistake. "Everybody is so excited about showing those numbers—again, the short-term focus—they fail to ask whether the plant really did save that much money, whether we really achieved those *gains*."

Many commercial kaizen activities bring in huge consulting fees, but they can be inherently dangerous and destructive. Don't "just do it!"

Honda BP leadership is seeking to help raise the maturity level of the supply base, although many North American companies would be comfortable doing a program that is designed to yield a five-year payback. Another difference between BP and other programs is that when companies have reached a level called self-reliance, the bar goes up a few more notches, because the kaizen culture means that the improvement challenge continues forever. "If it ain't broke, don't fix it" doesn't work in a kaizen culture.

Taking a leadership position as a customer means encouraging suppliers to explore new methods, like BP. For example, supplier study groups throughout the year work on various study topics. Once a year, the best participants meet to hear the top presentations from the best of Honda's supplier study groups. Meeting each month for 10 months, suppliers may even be competitors, but all look forward to their annual meeting for which over 300 suppliers show up. Although observers may think participants are presenting to management, they actually are speaking to other suppliers. Topics covered include administrative purchasing, productivity, and expansion issues.

LEADERSHIP METRICS

Metrics drive behavior, and metrics make the game fun. An old bowling story illustrates. We do many activities in which we don't keep score—driving, recreational weekend skiing, TV watching—but not keeping score in a game is like bowling with no scorecards and a sheet hanging over the pins. You may roll the ball and hear the pins drop, and you know you are bowling, but you soon tire of a game that has no end point, no trophy, no winner, and no runners-up.

Purchasing management at Honda has developed a comprehensive performance tracking, feedback, and history system for all

Figure 9.1　Performance Reports

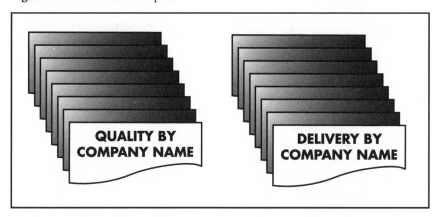

QUALITY BY
COMPANY NAME

DELIVERY BY
COMPANY NAME

purchasing materials. Supplier performance reporting at Marysville tracks eight key quality measures, eight key delivery measures, and detailed monthly performance for each supplier.

Managers also use a DTR (Domestic Trouble Report) system to highlight specific areas needing attention, such as labeling errors or packaging mistakes. Only by capturing problems as they occur and working with the supplier to find their root cause does Honda's extended enterprise continue to pursue its zero defects objectives.

Performance history for the life of the partnership is maintained for the same criteria—delivery and quality.

Suppliers are classified by commodity code—machine/casting, stampings, etc. Moreover, the system provides some room for subjective feedback, by specific part number, or by the purchasing manager's discretion.

Metrics that measure process, as well as the end result, work on both sides of the partnership, with the supplier and the customer. The list of excellence awards for purchasing and general company performance continues to grow, with some forms of recognition carrying more weight than others. The Baldrige Award, and even the process of preparing to submit an application, has value beyond winning or losing the award.

Figure 9.2   SPR System

```
┌─────────────────────────────────────────────────────────────┐
│                    *** COMMENTS ***                          │
│                                                              │
│ MAP-PPG:  THANK YOU FOR YOUR COOPERATION WITH ANY SCHEDULE   │
│           CHANGES MADE DURING THE MONTH. PLEASE SUBMIT JAPAN SUP- │
│           PLY PART INVENTORY ON FIRST DAY OF THE MONTH.      │
│ AEP-PPG:  THANK YOU FOR YOUR COOPERATION WITH ANY SCHEDULE   │
│           CHANGES MADE DURING THE MONTH. DTRS RETURNED LATE THIS │
│           MONTH TOTAL 2.                                     │
│ MAP-PPG:  THANKS FOR AN EXCELLENT MONTH.                     │
│ APS-PPG:  QUANTITY ERROR(S) RECORDED ON DTR(S) MIA-167.      │
│ ELP-PPG:  GOOD DELIVERY THIS MONTH. KEEP UP THE GOOD WORK.   │
│ MAP-QC:   GOOD MONTH.                                        │
│ ELP-QC:   OVERALL QUALITY FOR THE MONTH WAS GOOD. JOB WELL DONE. │
│           KEEP UP THE GOOD WORK.                             │
│                                                              │
│ NOTE: THIS REPORT DOES NOT REFLECT EVALUATION OF SHIPMENTS MADE │
│       DIRECTLY TO HONDA OF CANADA MANUFACTURING.             │
└─────────────────────────────────────────────────────────────┘
```

The Shingo Award and various state government quality awards get mixed reviews. Depending on which participants evaluate the award process and the criteria, some suppliers will choose not to invest their time seeking the medal.

LEADING BY EXAMPLE

Honda of America Purchasing has by three different methods been selected as the number one purchasing organization in the United States. Just as its suppliers compete for best-in-class awards, Honda aggressively pursues best-in-class ratings, medals, citations, and any other indicator that smacks of what Mr. Honda recognized as the only true racing spirit, being number one.

In 1995, *Purchasing* magazine awarded Honda's purchasing department its Medal of Excellence "for superb supplier development." Other specific excellence achievements recognized by the medal listed HAM's efforts in cost reduction, including productivity improvements shared 50/50 with the supplier, quality improvements, product research and development, and teaching self-reliance. Previous award winners include Hewlett Packard and Chrysler.

Two leading consulting firms, A. T. Kearney and McKinsey, have each ranked Honda purchasing as the best. A. T. Kearney scored Honda Purchasing 2.7 on a scale of 0 – 3 in February 1996, among 26 companies. The seven dimensions of procurement evaluated in the study were 1) Procurement strategy development process; 2) Procurement organization; 3) Strategic sourcing process; 4) Supplier management/development process; 5) Day-to-day purchasing and controlling process; 6) Performance measurement; and 7) Information management. The research study compiled information in the seven subject areas and conducted interviews and analysis for one full year before its 1996 conclusion.

Two items at that time were rated lower than the others—MRO procedures and information management. As a result, Honda launched its new information systems project, a comprehensive and on-line response to changing system needs, and a series of MRO organization and system initiatives.

Even among the best of the best, gaps appear. Compounding the performance challenge to purchasing and suppliers is the transition facing the entire profession. Procurement will face increasing pressure to change and assume new, more demanding roles. In a second evaluation, McKinsey's report warned that althrough leaders were aware of the imperative for change, major *implementation* gaps exist. In 1992, McKinsey also ranked Honda best of the best in its ten rating categories.

Finally, Honda continues to pursue top spots in internally recognized competitive market and efficiency studies, a reflection of the high performance levels of its supply base. They captured the 1997

J.D. Power and Associates Initial Quality Survey (IQS) honors for top vehicle in its class, an accurate assessment of quality performance directly from customers. In 1997, the Marysville Auto Plant was honored by J.D. Power as one of the top two car plants in the world, tying with the Ford plant in Atlanta for a platinum award.

The Call to Arms

"We *demand* suppliers be competitive; they [Honda] *help* them," says Gene Richter, currently head of IBM procurement, at the Arthur D. Little Colloquium on Supply Chain Management, during which executives from 12 companies representing $360 billion combined revenues met.[6]

For all the dollars North American companies spend on manpower and new equipment and elegant computer solutions, why do they not approach supplier development, whose proven payback to Honda is eight to one, with the same energy? In traditional American companies, purchasing takes a back-office position. Seize the opportunity, as have top contenders like Chrysler, Hewlett Packard, and Harley Davidson.

LEADERSHIP FOR THE PURCHASING PROFESSION

Leadership for the purchasing profession means hiring the best people, offering them an opportunity to understand other functions, and turning them loose. Give them the best tools—real time on-line supplier communications and tracking systems. Expect your purchasing associates to be out of the plant frequently, practicing the 3 A's. Invite your suppliers in frequently, and for long periods of time, because that kind of co-location arrangement—either as in-plants, or guest engineers—is the only approach that yields early, powerful design and cost benefits.

To raise the bar professionally, support professional development organizations, like NAPM (National Association of Purchasing Management), the CLM (Council of Logistics Management), and AME (the Association for Manufacturing Excellence) with money, information-sharing events, and executive-on-loan programs. Budget for professional attendance at least one yearly development conference, and more frequent seminars and events.

Reward excellence. Honda's tradition of sending all its executives out on post-Supplier Awards Conference plant visits, where purchasing leaders give awards to supplier associates, not managers or supervisors, is a powerful way to recognize essential associate contributions.

Benchmark your competition, remembering that solid competitors often reside outside your own industry walls. Open your plants to equivalent sharing initiatives. It is the only way to Raise the Bar.

10

The Gift of BP

You cannot be excellent all by yourself.

SIMPLICITY, CONCENTRATION, AND SPEED

Your business, whether it is automobile production, stamping, plastics, electronic assembly, publishing, or health care, can be an island of excellence—strong, but isolated, performing at levels well above its partners. Or, it can be a valued member of its own extended enterprise. Your passion must be to raise the bar in *all* your operations.

In business, everyone is a customer or a supplier to someone else. Each of us has the unique opportunity to make good products every time. Each of us has the unique opportunity to meet delivery commitments every time. And of course, each of us also has the opportunity of slipping back into low-margin operations.

Suppliers understand what the market and their customers want. Suppliers' challenge is finding the resources to raise the bar, as the great sensei Maruo says, a little higher each time.

Honda BP is a gift to organizations that step up to the opportunity to follow their passion. With what other methodology can a company expect to find immediate productivity gains in the 40 percent to 60 percent improvement range? And with what other improvement discipline can we find examples of operating personnel who understand and proceed without hesitation to redesign their workplace?

Only Honda BP has been proven among many kaizen-like approaches to have an enduring, yet changeable, impact on the workplace. Only BP practitioners can point to a number of grafted and nurtured approaches grown from suppliers' early successes, like those of Parker Hannifin, TRW, and Donnelly Corporation, which have taken root and blossomed into a new variety of home-grown continuous improvement. Only the true BP experts—Reynosa's Rocio and Mary in Parker's Batesville, Mississippi, plant, and hundreds of others who have experienced the empowerment of BP—can speak to the future of manufacturing at higher levels of quality and leanness than ever dreamed by Henry Ford or Frederick Taylor.

BP is a simple methodology that has few requirements for successful performance. But one absolute essential to beginning the process is to go in *gemba* (the actual place). Many years ago, purchasing and other "support" professionals were discouraged from visiting their own shop floor or that of suppliers; likewise, suppliers sent sales personnel to "seal the deal." What happened next followed a well-worn scenario, as leagues of expeditors, coordinators, schedulers, and occasional plant managers rushed to fill the gaps. Growth was painful and uncontrolled at best.

Honda BP proposes intense focus on the business at hand, winning the race through teamwork, simplicity, concentration, and speed. Second place is losing, and for each of the over 300,000 U.S.-based smaller suppliers to take a place at the starting line and finish the race, they must be ready on time, and be supported by the best pit crew they can attract.

THE ROCK AND THE SHOE

If you have had the experience of walking with a small stone in your shoe, you will remember that, although you can ignore the discomfort and hobble on a bit, eventually you will stop, remove the shoe, and find that rock. Poor performing businesses are the rock in the shoe. Although they may be tolerated for several miles, eventually their business partners will stop by the side of the road to locate the trouble. And when that irritating pebble is discovered, it is removed *forever*.

North America's gifts to industry include a long line of pioneers and unsung heroes, from Francis Cabot Lowell's dream of the first fully integrated textile operation on the banks of the Charles River and Paul Moody's engineering expertise that cast the dream in iron, to Taylor, Ford, Sloan, Deming and Juran, and dozens of as-yet-undiscovered geniuses.

Now, with the gift of BP, the voice of thousands of associates is heard for the first time—press operators, engineers, assemblers, material handlers, schedulers, maintenance people. Each BP activity strengthens their powerful voice in the business of making things.

Live your passion in *gemba*. Let your fingers memorize the shape of the product. Teach your eyes to see the perfection of an excellent workplace. Learn to listen and hear the sounds of quiet work; teach your ears to hear the silence. Respect the quiet of work being done well and smoothly. Raise your voice as a leader, a sensei, who knows the possibilities, whose patience and commitment to the best raises the efforts of all the people in The Race—your partners, your competitors, your pit crew, and even the spectators.

Listen to them. Take the gift.

Appendix
The BP Toolbox

Part One: Glossary (Definitions and Tools)

Part Two: Sample BP Documents

Part Three: For more information

A. On the extended enterprise and proven partnering practices, see *Breakthrough Partnering*, by Patricia E. Moody, (New York: John Wiley and Sons, © 1993) ISBN 0471-131-997

B. On various manufacturing excellence practices, including teaming, quality basics and quality circles, sales and operations planning, how to build manufacturing flexibility, next generation manufacturing and the extended enterprise, and kaizen practices, see *Leading Manufacturing Excellence*, by (New York: John Wiley and Sons, © 1997) ISBN 0-471-16341-4

C. On basic, proven approaches to quality methods, see *What Is Total Quality Control?* by Kaoru Ishikawa, (New York: Prentice Hall, 1989) ISBN 0-13-952441-X

D. On innovation and best practices in manufacturing, see *Target* magazine, published by the Assn. for Mfg. Excellence. Patricia E. Moody, Editor, 847-520-3282, fax 847-520-0163.

E. Talk with the authors:
Dave Nelson, Rick Mayo, or Patricia E. Moody – PwdbyHonda@aol.com

PART ONE, GLOSSARY

BP—Best Position, Best Productivity, Best Product, Best Price, Best Partners

Cells—The grouping of various machines, for example, lathes, presses, grinders, polishers, that perform different operations into a layout that permits parts to be completed in a one-at-a-time, or batches of one, process flow. The machines are typically laid out in a U-shaped cell to eliminate wasted movement for the operator and the materials.

Changeover—Time required to prepare a machine or a line to produce a different kind of part. Changeover time may mean cleaning or breaking down a paint machine, for example, to run a different color; or it may mean changing the die on a press to run a different stamping or a different material.

Control Chart—A visual method that displays data distribution against a calculated upper limit and lower limit. Statistically derived, this chart usually depicts the ideal or average performance of a process against unacceptable performance limits.

COPDS—Clean up, Organize, Pick up, Discipline, Safety.

Cycle time—Time required to complete one operation, for example, cycle time for painting is two hours.

Deming's Circle—Plan, Do, Check, Act. Visually, a wheel diagram used to describe one approach to problem-solving and continuous improvement.

Five S's—*Seiri* – separate materials and tools from waste; *seiton* – arrange and identify tools; *seiso* – clean-up; *seiketsu* – daily clean-up; and *shitsuke* – continuous practice of clean-up, etc.

Flow chart—A visual representation that uses common symbols to depict a process. A triangle indicates a decision point, an oval is start or stop, a rectangle indicates a processing step or transaction, and a square indicates storage or inventory.

Histogram—A visual method of displaying the distribution of data, for example, in a class of 40 students, grade distribution might appear as follows:

Figure A.1 Histogram: 3 As, 15 Bs, 20 Cs, 1 D, and 1 F

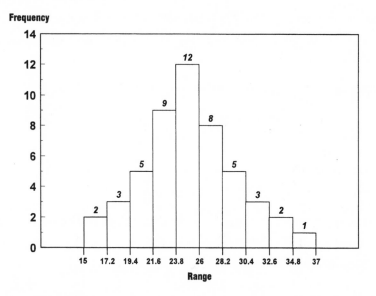

Just-in-time (JIT)—Producing and delivering the number of parts required by customers just as they are required by the customer order or by the next downstream process.

Kaizen—Literally, in Japanese, "to make better."

Kanban—Literally, in Japanese, "cards"; cards or labels attached to a container that signal upstream production processes to make more, and refill the container; keystone of a pull (versus MRP push) system.

Leadtime—Calculated as throughput, plus move, plus wait time, leadtime frequently and incorrectly describes the time quoted to a customer during which he must wait for a particular part.

MRP (Material Requirements Planning)—A system derived by IBM and Oliver Wight, now computerized, from Time-Phased Reorder Point Planning, in which a high-level demand, driven by a forecast or a customer order, is broken down through a computer algorithm called the Bill of Material, into time-phased requirements.

Pareto Analysis—A visual method to display and study large amounts of data, typically in a vertical bar graph, by frequency of occurrence.

Poke-yoke—Mistake-proofing a process or an operation.

Pull—A system that drives production operations by cascading customer requirements upstream to all processes.

Queue time—Wait time. In traditional production environments this waste time amounts to 80 percent of all leadtime.

Scatter diagram—Another method to study the pattern or distribution of data describing various events. Typically, data is displayed on a scatter diagram plotted against two axes.

Figure A.2   Scatter Diagram

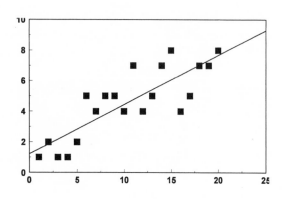

Seven Wastes—Over-production, idle time, delivery, waste in the work itself, inventory waste, wasted operator movement, waste from reject parts.

Single-piece flow—The sequence of making one entire product at a time, before the next product is begun, by putting a single piece through all its operations.

Spaghetti chart—A map used to illustrate the movement of an operator or a part as it completes various production operations.

Standard deviation, or sigma (σ)—Used as a measure of the distribution of a process or a sample.

Suggestion system—A systematic approach to encouraging, and rewarding participation by the workforce in the solutions that improve productivity.

Takt time—From the German "baton" or "beat"; in production planning, the calculation of takt time is available production time divided by the rate of customer demand. Takt time sets the production rate following customer needs; if the customer demand for a part is 200 per day, and the factory produces at the rate of 400 minutes per day, the calculated takt time is 2 minutes.

Target cost—The total cost of production, labor, materials, overhead, and profit, plus research and development, for which the customer expects to pay.

Throughput time—The total time required for a product to complete all its operations, from raw materials to the customer.

The 14 BP Techniques—

1. QCL items, 5 P's, 5 Whys
2. Efficient layouts
3. Production leveling
4. Visual controls
5. Pull System (kanban)
6. Poke-yoke
7. One-to-one production
8. Reduction of leadtime
9. Proper tools and processes
10. Standardization
11. Improving supplier quality
12. Preventive maintenance
13. Quick die/mold change
14. Just-in-time

The 3A's—Go to the Actual place, study the Actual parts, then understand the Actual situation.

Visual management, visibility management, visual control(s) —A methodology or philosophy that simplifies and clarifies the workplace by making operations, tools, and parts clear to operators by their visual placement and signaling in the workplace.

PART TWO, SAMPLE BP DOCUMENTS

Figure A.3   12-Month Basic BP Schedule

12-MONTH BASIC SCHEDULE

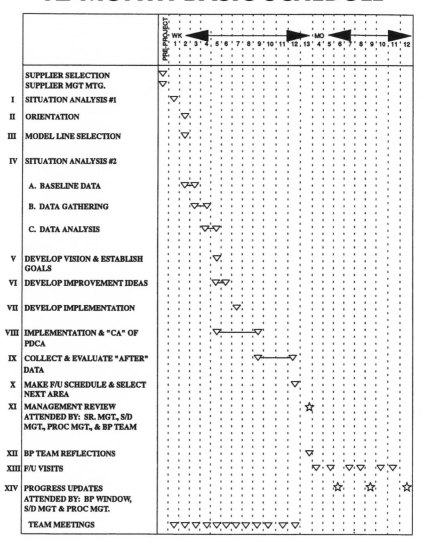

Figure A.4   Checklist for meeting with Supplier Management before beginning BP

Supplier Management Meeting

After the supplier has been selected a meeting is scheduled
between their top management and Procurement/SD management.

One of the first items addressed in this meeting is for the Honda
representatives to describe the BP project to the supplier's
management and ask them is they are interested in participating.
As mentioned earlier, this is a **voluntary program** and will not
be forced on a supplier.

If the supplier agrees to participate, the meeting continues with
the following major areas being covered:

A. Need for top management support throughout the project

B. Basic philosophy of a 50/50 sharing of manufacturing cost

C. Basic schedule of Procurement involvement for cost negotiation
    −No negotiation to take place until the 6-month point in the project.

D. Manpower commitment for the entire 12-month project
    − 1–2 people full time. The normal duties of these people need to
       be assigned to other people for the duration of the project.
    − Entry level to middle management in the following disciplines
       are preferred:
         Supervisory
         Process engineering
         Maintenance
         Production/inventory control
         Purchasing

E. Need to continue on with the project and expand the skills learned
    throughout the production floor and through the other departments
    in the facility

F. Need to set up an organization to support continuous improvement

G. Need to set up systems to maintain the employee involvement
    enthusiasm developed during the project. This can include:
    −Suggestion systems
    −Quality circle activities
    −Communication channels

Figure A.5   Checklist for performing Situation Analysis #1

I. Situation Analysis #1

Definition: **To separate something into its parts in order to study it or better understand it**

Situation Analysis #1 is the gathering of all information available at Honda about a supplier and the parts they supply. This analysis is performed by the Honda BP team before their first visit to the supplier and repeated at each facility that receives parts from the supplier.

Areas Analyzed:

1. **Lines at Manufacturing Facility**
   - View parts being assembled to automobile.
   - Understand Fit/Function to car.
   - Discuss parts with associates and team leaders to find out any problems, concerns, requests for changes, etc.
2. **Material Service**
   - Discuss delivery situation with associates.
   - Further review packaging situation.
3. **Auto Parts Quality (APQ)**
   Meet with supplier associates to discuss quality situation.
   - PPM levels—current and trend
   - Potential part changes
   - Current/past problems
   - Response to quality problems
4. **Parts Procurement Group (PPG)**
   Meet with supplier associates to understand delivery situation.
   - Delivery PPM level - current and trend
   - Logistics of parts (where and how they are delivered). If MEI, Visit.
   - Current/past problems
   - Applications of supplier parts
   - Response to delivery problems/requests (flexibility)
5. **Procurement**
   Meet with supplier associates to understand procurement situations.
   - Review and understand quotes.
   - What type of pricing is used? Target or formula?
   - What has been the supplier competitive history?
   - What is procurement's short/long-term strategy for the supplier and/or individual parts?
6. **Quality Engineering Department (QED)**
   Meet with supplier associates to understand engineering situation.
   - Understand warranty situation of suppliers parts.
   - Understand open/potential design change/manufacturing instructions involving supplier parts.

Figure A.6   Checklist for Supplier BP Orientation

II. Orientation

One of the first activities conducted when the Honda BP team arrives at the supplier is BP orientation. This orientation is to provide the supplier members and management with a basic overview of the project and the major philosophies and tools used during it.

List of items discussed during this orientation:

1. **What is BP?**

2. **Basic Schedule**
    – Set the date for the final evaluation.

3. **Logistics of Project:**
    A. Days of the week to meet
    B. Start/finish times daily
    C. Attire
    D. Requirements of meeting room
    E. Phone and fax
    F. Agendas and documentation
    G. If union facility, what rules to follow
    H. Discuss use of stopwatches, videos, 35mm pictures, and slides
    I. Safety equipment

4. **Need for management support.**
    A. Instill the "vision" to all associates
    B. Support by example—"forks in the road"
    C. Resources:
        – Maintenance   – Engineering   – Purchasing
    D. Recognition

5. **Basic philosophies:**
    A. Associate involvement
    B. Minimum investment—Intro to Phase II
    C. Raw material utilization (yield.
    D. Spec BP
    E. Identify and eliminate waste (7 wastes)
    F. COPDS (kitchen, wall side, visibility, closet strategies)
    G. 3A's
    H. Deming's Circle (PDCA).
    I. 8 categories—25 items
    J. Displaced associates

6. **Basic tools:**
    A. Calculations
    B. Forms

Figure A.7 Five Principles for Problem-Solving

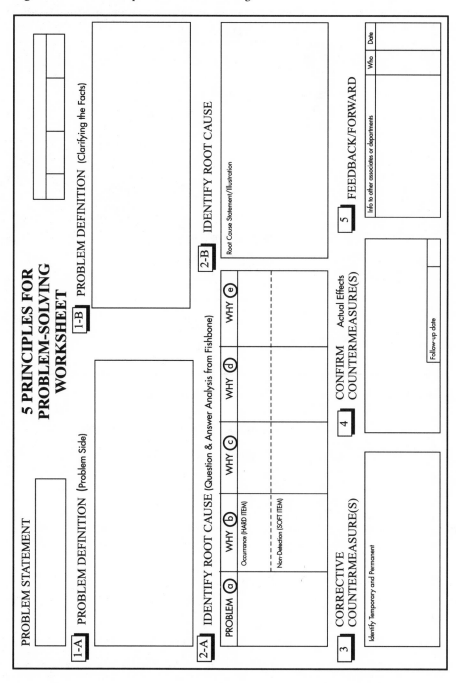

Figure A.8   Pull System with Kanban Containers

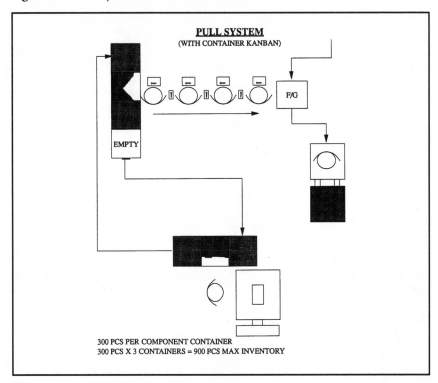

Figure A.9   Normal and Maximum Range of Motion Diagram

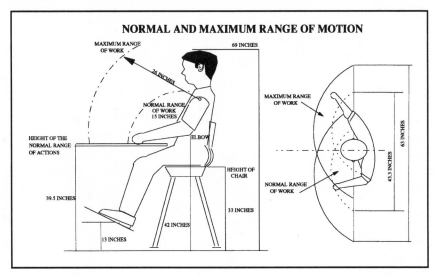

Figure A.10   Building The JIT Pyramid

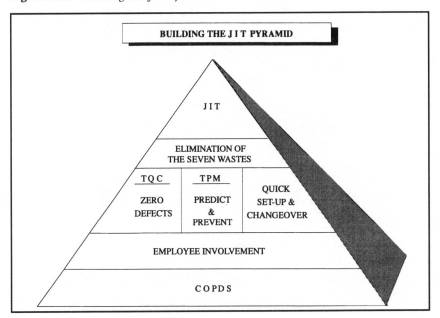

Figure A.11   The Basics of JIT Production

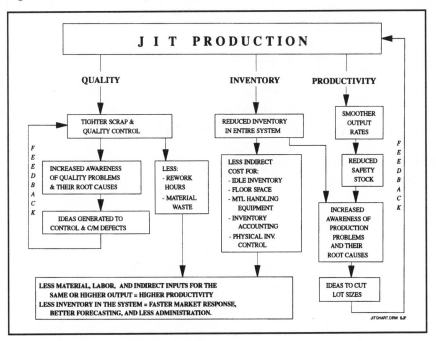

Figure A.12   Baseline Data Examples – line balance, production efficiency, production per manhour, labor $ per part calculations

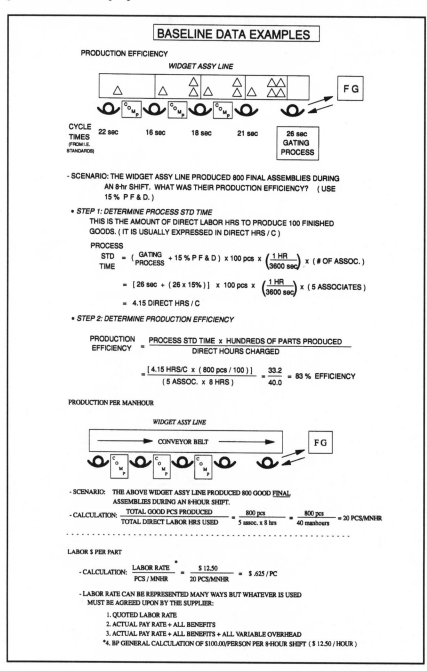

Figure A.13 Time Study Analysis Sheet

TIME STUDY ANALYSIS SHEET

LINE/PART _____ ASSOCIATE _____ DATE _____

No.	MOTION	T I M E						Secs or 100ths				$\bar{x}$
		1	2	3	4	5	6	7	8	9	10	$\bar{x}$
	TOTAL PROCESS CYCLE	18.7	19.8	22.1	24.0	20.9	19.2	22.7	23.1	25.4	22.1	**21.8**
	PROCESS SEGMENTS											
	1. PICK UP PART, PLACE	3.7	3.9	4.2	4.1	4.2	4.2	4.4	4.0	4.1	3.8	4.1
	2. M/C CYCLE TIME	10.2	10.2	10.1	10.2	10.1	10.2	10.2	10.3	10.2	10.1	10.2
	3. REMOVE, INSPECT, PASS	7.5	8.0	7.6	7.8	7.7	7.4	8.1	8.1	7.5	8.2	7.8
												22.1

Figure A.14　Reject Tracking Sheet

REJECT TRACKING SHEET
INTEGRATED WIDGET ASSY LINE

PART # __74891-S02-A010-M1__
DATE ____4 - 20 - 92____
SHIFT _____1ST_____

REJECT \ HOUR	1	2	3	4	5	6	7	8	TOTALS
SPLAY	III	II	III		II		卌		15
STREAKS	II	II	II			I	III	I	11
SHORT SHOT						I			1
OVERPACK		I	I			II		I	5
GATE BLUSH	I		I	I	I				4
STRESS MARK	III	II	IIII	II	III	I	III	I	19
TOTALS	9	7	11	3	7	4	11	3	55

TOTAL PIECES PRODUCED = 855
REJECT % = 55 ÷ 855 X 100 = 6.4%

Figure A.15 Data Analysis Checklist

<u>**Data Analysis.**</u>

Now that all the data has been collected the team must carefully analyze and put it into an easily understood form. The following is a list of commonly used BP Data Forms and examples.

1. <u>**Line Balance Charts**</u> - These charts are developed from the time studies and graphically illustrate how well distributed the work load is on the model line. During the project the team will try to get the line balance as high as possible. Any line balance below 85% is considered unacceptable and must be improved.

2. <u>**Make Pareto Charts**</u>
   Definition: A chart used to separate the significant few from the trivial many.

   The team uses Pareto Charts to direct them where to concentrate their efforts for maximum benefits. Although three months appears to be a long period of time, the team cannot be wasting time on trivial issues.

3. <u>**Lost Time Graphs**</u> - These graphs are used to show how well the Model Line is performing according to a theoretical optimum. This graph is developed from time study data, company policies, and lineside observation.

   After establishing the optimum and actual line performance the team attempts to identify all the reasons for the difference.

4. <u>**Idea Tracking Sheets**</u> - The team takes all the ideas that have been submitted and organizes them on the Idea Tracking Sheet. These sheets are created so that none of the ideas are lost throughout the project and they make excellent follow-up tools.

   A good way to increase/maintain the enthusiasm of Model Line associates is to post the Idea Tracking Sheets in their area. In this way they can monitor the idea's progress and also add any further ideas they may come up with.

Figure A.16　DATA Analysis Calculations

DATA ANALYSIS CALCULATIONS

LINE CAPACITY FOR BP PURPOSES, WE USE A VERY SIMPLE CALCULATION TO CALCULATE LINE CAPACITY. TAKE THE AVAILABLE SECONDS PER SHIFT, DIVIDE BY THE GATING CYCLE TIME, AND MULTIPLY THIS BY A 90% FACTOR.

WIDGET ASSY LINE EXAMPLE:

$26{,}700S \div 26S = 1{,}026 \text{ PCS} \times .90 = 924 \text{ PCS}$

LEADTIME THE TOTAL TIME REQUIRED TO PRODUCE A PART AFTER AN ORDER HAS BEEN RECEIVED. THIS TIME IS THROUGHPUT TIME PLUS:

1. TIME REQUIRED TO OBTAIN RAW MATERIAL AND COMPONENT PARTS.
2. SCHEDULING DELAYS TO GET THE PART INTO THE PRODUCTION LINE OR MACHINE.

Figure A.17   Line Balance Chart Example

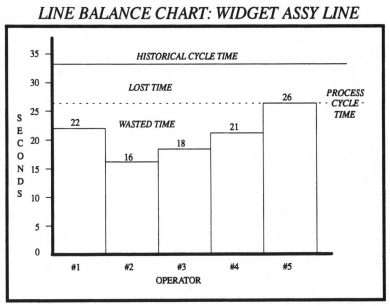

LINE BALANCE CHART: WIDGET ASSY LINE

CALCULATIONS:

- LINE BALANCE = $\dfrac{22 + 16 + 18 + 21 + 26}{26 \times 5}$ = $\dfrac{103}{130}$ = 79%

- WASTED TIME =   130 s - 103 s = 27 s

    (NOTICE THAT WASTED TIME (27 s) IS LONGER THAN THE PROCESS CYCLE (26 s)
    WHICH INDICATES THAT BY SHIFTING RESPONSIBILITIES, ONE PERSON COULD BE
    ELIMINATED FROM THE LINE WITHOUT INCREASING THE PROCESS CYCLE TIME.)

- HISTORICAL CYCLE TIME = $\dfrac{\text{AVAILABLE SECONDS PER SHIFT}}{\text{AVERAGE PCS PER SHIFT}}$

    = $\dfrac{26{,}700 \text{ s}^{*}}{800 \text{ pcs}}$ = 33.37 SECOND CYCLE TIME

    * = 480 MINUTE SHIFT MINUS 35 MINUTES FOR BREAKS, MTG, & C.O.P.

Figure A.18   Reject Pareto Chart

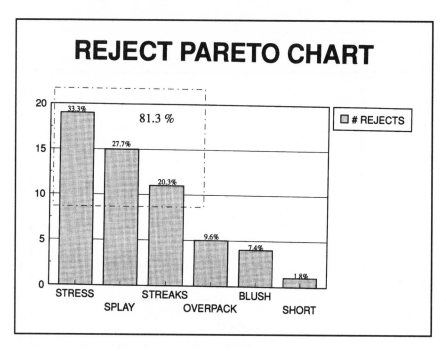

Figure A.19   BP Idea Tracking Chart

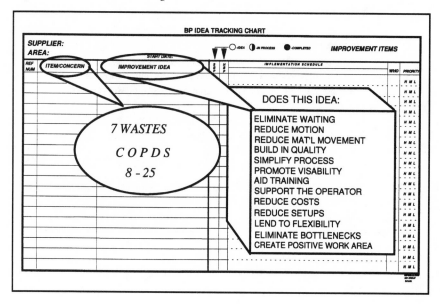

Figure A.20 Implementation Checklist

Develop Implementation Plan

After the team has developed all of their major improvement ideas, they must develop an implementation plan. This plan differs from the schedules on the Idea Tracking Sheet because of the complexity of the change. An example of a major improvement would be a major layout change in the model area.

The development of the Major Improvement Ideas Implementation Plan can be broken down into 3 main areas:

1. **Brainstorming to determine each specific item that must be completed.**

2. **Researching to find out what support area's assistance will be required to complete each item and the lead time required.**

3. **Laying out all the items scheduled on a Gantt chart.**

Figure A.21   Management Review Checklist

Management Review

Usually around the twelfth or thirteenth week of the project the team will present the results of the project to both Honda and the supplier's management.

These results are usually told in a story form with the main items as follows:

1. Brief outline of supplier company.
2. Selection of Model Line.
3. Brief description of Model Line products & processes.
4. Description of Baseline Data Collected.
5. Description of S/A findings and establishment of goals.
6. Idea Development.
7. Implementation.
8. Comparison of Baseline & After Data.
9. Overall Manufacturing Cost Impact to the Model Line
10. Description of follow-up schedule and schedule for the next Model Line.
11. A brief description of the impact of the BP project to the members.

The presentation is usually followed by a question and answer session for Honda & supplier management and a Model Line Tour.

Notes

1   Tetsuo Sakiya, *Honda Motor, the Men, the Management, the Machines* (Tokyo and New York: Kodansha International, 1982).

2   James Treece, "Just-too-much single-sourcing spurs Toyota purchasing review." *Automotive News,* March 3, 1997.

3   "Toyota Factories in Japan Grind to a Halt." *Wall Street Journal,* February 4, 1997.

4   Valerie Reitman, "Toyota's Fast Rebound After Fire." *Wall Street Journal,* May 18, 1997, pp. 1, A16.

5   James P. Womack and Daniel T. Jones, *Lean Thinking* (New York: Simon and Schuster, 1996).

6   James A. Welch and N. Laddie Cook, "Supply Chain Management," *PRISM,* 3rd Quarter, 1994.

Index